Ju
92
ML7A   MEIR, GOLDA.
        Davidson, Margaret.
               The Golda Meir story.
        Rev. ed.

Ju
92
ML7A   Davidson, Margaret.
               The Golda Meir story.
        Rev. ed.

Temple Israel Library
Minneapolis, Minn.

Please sign your full name on the above card.

Return books promptly to the Library or Temple Office.

Fines will be charged for overdue books or for damage or loss of same.

THE GOLDA MEIR STORY

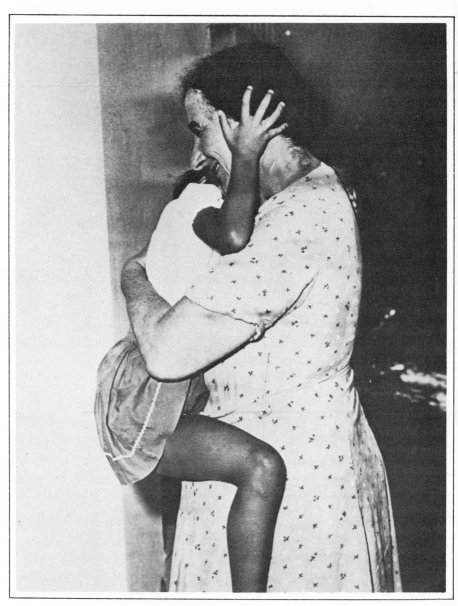

Golda hugs one of her five grandchildren. "They are the greatest joy of my life," she commented many times.

The
Golda Meir Story

by *Margaret Davidson*

REVISED EDITION

Charles Scribner's Sons
New York

To Ruth,
with all my love

Copyright © 1976, 1981 Margaret Davidson

Library of Congress Cataloging in Publication Data
Davidson, Margaret, date
The Golda Meir story.
Bibliography: p.
Includes index.
SUMMARY: A biography of Golda Meir, whose
childhood memories of Russia helped her work to
establish the independent state of Israel.
1. Meir, Golda Mabovitz, 1898-   —Juvenile
literature. 2. Prime ministers—Israel—Biography—
Juvenile literature. 3. Zionists—Biography—
Juvenile literature. [1. Meir, Golda Mabovitz,
1898-   2. Statesmen] I. Title.
DS126.6.M42D38   1981   956.94′05′0924   [B]   [92]
ISBN 0-684-16877-4   80-26970

1 3 5 7 9 11 13 15 17 19   V/C   20 18 16 14 12 10 8 6 4 2

Printed in the United States of America

photo credits: Zionist Archives and Library (frontis-
piece; 122d, bottom; 122e; 122f); Wide World Photos
(122a; 122c); Israel Government Press Office (122b);
Consulate General of Israel in New York (122d, top).

Contents

1

The Almost-Pogrom

It was the silence that scared Golda most.

The time was mid-afternoon, and the street should have been filled with all sorts of everyday sounds— people talking, dogs barking, babies crying, peddlers shouting their wares. But it wasn't. Now only one sound broke the strange silence—the ringing *clang, clang, clang* of hammers hitting nails.

What was going on? Golda didn't know, and no one would tell her. Whenever she asked, her mother just said to be quiet. Well, whatever it was, Golda knew one thing. She didn't like it at all!

It had all started an hour ago with a knock on their door. When Golda's father answered it, a neighbor was standing there. "Come outside for a moment, will you, Moshe?" he said. His voice was quiet and his words ordinary. But Golda's mother had looked up sharply. And even four-year-old Golda could feel the sudden tension in the room.

When Moshe Mabovitch came back inside his face was set and pale. He and his wife whispered for a few moments. Then Golda saw her mother's face go pale, too.

"There are some old planks around back," Moshe said. "I'll get them." He put on his jacket and started outside again. Golda's mother threw a shawl over her shoulders and started to follow.

"Mama . . ." Golda began.

Bluma Mabovitch whirled around, a surprised look on her face—as if she'd forgotten Golda was there at all. "Please, Mama," Golda begged, "can I come outside with you?"

Golda could tell by the look on her face that her mother was going to say no. Then—perhaps because she saw how confused and frightened her daughter was—she changed her mind. "All right, Goldie, get your coat," she said. "But outside is one thing. Wandering is another. I want you to stay right by the front door. Do you understand? Not a foot away."

So now Golda stood by the door, growing more and more scared by the minute. Nearby her father was busy hammering. All up and down the street other men were doing the same thing—nailing heavy boards across the windows and doors of their homes.

But no, Golda noticed, not everyone. In front of

some of the houses people were just standing, staring. They didn't look unfriendly exactly. But they didn't look friendly, either.

Without really thinking about it, Golda accepted this. These people were neighbors. She and they both lived together in the city of Kiev. But she knew that somehow they were different. Long ago Mama had told her not to mingle with them. "Some of them are kind enough," she'd explained. "But some are not— not to us, anyway. So it's best to stay apart."

Golda had been puzzled by this. She still was. But now wasn't the time to think about that. There was too much else going on! Just then Moshe stopped hammering to wipe the sweat off his face. He saw Golda, and bent to pick up a long stick from the pile of lumber at his feet.

"Here," he said, thrusting it into her hand. "Use it if you have to."

Use it? How? And *why?* Golda stared at the stick. It felt so rough and heavy in her hand that she wanted to drop it. But Papa had given it to her, and somehow that was very important right now. So she clutched the old stick so hard the rough edges bit into her palm.

Bluma and some of the other women were standing in a little group nearby, whispering among themselves. Golda tried to hear what they were saying. But their voices were too low. No matter how hard she tried she couldn't catch even a word.

Maybe if she were a little closer. Slowly, slowly,

she inched toward the group of whispering women. Finally she could hear a part of what they were saying.

"When do you think it will start?"

". . . usually about sundown . . ."

Golda looked up at the sky. The sun was already sinking behind the buildings at the far end of the street.

"Yes," another woman said, making a spitting motion with her lips. "They are always more comfortable in the dark."

"Did you hear about the pogrom in . . ."

". . . yes, and even the synagogue was burned . . ."

"But it wasn't as bad as the pogrom last year. Eleven people died before that was . . ."

"Boards—what good will a few boards do?"

"That's right," another woman agreed. "Boards didn't stop the pogrom there."

Golda shook her head in confusion. She could hear snatches of what they were saying, but not enough to understand what was really going on. And there was that word they used again and again. *Pogrom.* What did it mean? What did *any* of this mean?

Her father finished nailing the last board in place. Just then Golda's sister Shaina came home. "Hurry," Moshe said. "Get inside, all of you."

There were five people in the Mabovitch family— Golda's mother and father, her teenage sister Shaina, and her younger sister Zipka. Once inside, they all huddled together in the one room that was their home.

The room was always dark. Now it was almost pitch-black. But Moshe wouldn't let them light a lamp—or even a candle. "It's safer this way," he said. So everyone just sat . . . and waited.

Suppertime came, but Moshe wouldn't let Bluma build a fire in the stove. "They might see the smoke," he said. So Bluma put some cold potatoes and a half loaf of black bread on the table. Golda played with her potato for a few minutes. But then she shoved it away. She just wasn't hungry. No one else was either. They were all too tense to eat.

"What's that?" Shaina whispered a few minutes later. But it was only a horse and rider going by. An hour passed. Then the sound of shouting broke the silence. "Shhh!" Bluma commanded—although no one was talking. Then they heard the sound of laughter, too. It must be a group of men on their way to the tavern in the next street.

Finally Golda heard her father sigh. "I think you can light a candle now, Bluma. It's too late for them to come."

Bluma lit a candle. Then she turned to Golda. "Come along," she said briskly. "It's long past time you should be in bed."

But Golda wasn't tired. As a matter of fact, she'd never felt more wide awake. She had so many questions to ask. One above all she just had to have an answer for.

"Papa," she asked, "what does pogrom mean?"

For what seemed a long time her father said nothing. Had he forgotten about her and her question? Then he patted his lap. "Come here, Goldie," he said. Finally when she was settled, he asked, "Do you know who the czar is?"

Golda frowned. When was Papa going to answer *her* question? But he was waiting for her to speak, so she nodded a little doubtfully. "I think so. He lives in a great big palace, and . . . and when he goes for trips he rides in a big gold coach!"

Moshe smiled. "Yes. What else do you know about him?"

"Well . . ." Golda thought hard for a moment. "He . . . he tells us what to do!"

"That's right, Golda." Now her father wasn't smiling. "He tells everyone in Russia what to do, and what not to do. Well, Golda, this Czar Nicholas of ours is not a very nice man. And neither were the czars who came before him. For centuries they have loved two things above all else—money and power. But they haven't wanted to share these things. So most of the people in Russia today have very little money, and even less power.

"Naturally most people aren't very happy about this. But the czar doesn't want them to blame *him,* so he tells them it's somebody else's fault. And who does he blame? Us—the Jews. He says that all the poverty and misery and disease in Russia today are *our* fault."

"*Our* fault?" Golda asked.

"Yes. Your fault and mine—and the fault of all

the other Jews of Russia. It doesn't make very much sense, since we're poorer than most of the others. But ignorant people are always ready to blame their troubles on *someone.*''

"Why?" Golda asked now.

"You mean why are we blamed—and not someone else?"

Golda nodded. She guessed that was what she meant.

"The main reason, I think," Moshe answered, "is that we're different. For one thing we have a different religion. Most people in Russia are Christians. We have some different customs, too. Sometimes we wear different clothes. We even speak a different language when we are alone."

Golda nodded again. She knew that they all spoke Yiddish in the family. Suddenly she had an idea. "If I speak Russian would they like me?"

Moshe Mabovitch laughed, but his laughter had a bitter edge to it. "If only it were that simple, Goldie. But it's not. Old hatreds just don't go away that easily—especially not with the czar and his people telling new lies all the time."

Golda stirred restlessly on her father's lap. All this was very interesting. But he hadn't answered her question yet.

"Papa," she asked again, "what is a pogrom?"

Moshe sighed. "Do you remember when I told you how poor most people in Russia are?"

"Yes."

"Well, poor people are often angry—angry at the misery in their lives. Sometimes this anger can cause them to strike out, especially if they are encouraged to. And that's what the czar and his kind have been doing in Russia for hundreds of years. Encouraging ignorant people to act out their misery and their hate. Encouraging them to become mobs."

Golda wrinkled her forehead. "Is *that* what a pogrom is?" she interrupted. "A mob?"

Her father nodded. "Yes, mobs that sometimes run wild through the streets, smashing up Jewish stores and burning down Jewish homes . . ."

"And sometimes killing, too," Shaina added.

"Hush!" Bluma snapped. "She's too young for talk like that."

"I think not," said Moshe. "For she must live here, too."

Golda opened her mouth to ask another question, but instead she yawned. That yawn was followed by another. And then another. So many things had happened today. Golda's eyes began to close. Moments later she was fast asleep, her head nestled against the rough wool of her father's jacket.

She slept quietly for a few hours, but then she had a bad dream. In the dream the sound of hammers was growing louder, and louder, and louder . . .

Golda must have cried out, for she woke to find Mama standing by her bed. "Go back to sleep, Goldie," she said softly. "And don't worry. You'll forget. You'll forget soon."

But Bluma was wrong. Golda never forgot. The sound of those hammers and the sight of those planks would stay with her for the rest of her life. "If there is any logical explanation necessary for the direction which my life has taken," Golda was to say many years later, "maybe this is it—the desire and the determination to save Jewish children, four and five years old, from a similar scene and a similar experience."

2

"I Am Going to America"

The year was 1903. And Golda's first memory was of a pogrom that didn't happen. She also had other memories of those early years in the city of Kiev. For one thing she remembered the weather. Of course it couldn't always have been so bone-chillingly cold, but that's how she remembered it. She also remembered the Cossacks—those fierce and frightening special soldiers of the czar—and how when they came galloping through the streets everyone would scatter.

Most of all she remembered being hungry. Like the cold, hunger seemed to be an almost constant part of life.

Golda's father was a master carpenter. He could make almost anything with his long-fingered hands. He was especially proud of an icebox he'd built. It was one of the very first in Kiev. Too bad they had so little food to put inside it.

It wasn't that Moshe Mabovitch had trouble finding work. There were many rich families who needed the services of a good carpenter. No, finding work wasn't the problem. The problem was getting paid for it.

Often he was paid only part of what he'd been promised. Sometimes he wasn't paid at all. And there was nothing he could do about it. "Remember," he was told more than once, "it is a privilege you live here. Not a right."

Which was true. Kiev was outside the Pale of Settlement—an area near the western border of Russia where most Jews were forced to live. Only those who had special talents were allowed to live outside the Pale. Moshe Mabovitch was one of them. Because of his talent as a carpenter, he had been given a special permit to live and work in Kiev, the capital city of the Ukraine. But that permit could be taken away at any moment, for wherever he lived, a Jew was always a second-class citizen.

But then one day, not long after the almost-pogrom, something wonderful happened. Or at least it was the promise of something wonderful. The carpenters of Kiev were invited to bid on a very big job. A rich nobleman who lived near town wanted a whole houseful of ornate furniture made.

Each bid—the description of how the carpenter

would handle the job and how much he would charge for it—was to be by number only. "So only my qualifications will be judged," Moshe explained excitedly to Bluma, "not *what* I am!"

For the next few evenings Moshe sat hunched over the kitchen table, planning what materials he would use and calculating costs. "Only the best wood," he muttered, "and the highest quality nails . . ." And yet he wanted to submit a low bid—for that would be very important, too.

Finally he was finished. "I won't make very much money," he explained to Bluma. "Actually, I'll make almost nothing at all. But that isn't what matters. This man has many rich and important friends. If I do a good job, surely he will recommend me to some of them."

Moshe's eyes began to dance. "Just think, Bluma! Maybe soon I will be able to set myself up in a little shop, and even hire a full-time helper!"

And it seemed that Moshe's dreams were going to come true, for a few days later he was notified. The job was his!

How he worked then! All day and long into the night he sawed and shaped the pieces of wood into chairs and tables and chests. Then slowly, carefully, he carved their surfaces into intricate patterns. He sanded the pieces until they were satin smooth. Then he polished them until they gleamed.

At last even Moshe had to admit there was nothing more he could do. The next morning everyone watched as he and a helper loaded the furniture onto a cart. "Careful there! Careful!" he cried again and again. Finally every piece was snugly in place.

He climbed into the driver's seat and picked up the reins. How tall and handsome he looked sitting there! And happy. Now, as he waved good-bye, he broke into the words of a gay Yiddish folksong. Moshe Mabovitch loved to sing—especially when he was in a mood like this. Golda could still hear his voice as he rounded the corner at the far end of the street.

A different man came home.

"What is it? What happened?" Bluma cried, as soon as she saw his face.

Slowly Moshe took off his coat. He hung it neatly on a hook by the door. Then he slumped in a chair. It was only early afternoon, but Golda thought she had never seen her father look so tired.

"What happened?" Bluma cried again. "Didn't they like your furniture?"

"Oh, they liked it all right . . ." Moshe's voice trailed off.

"Well, then?"

"It was my name they didn't like."

Now slowly, haltingly, Moshe told them what had happened. Everything had been a wonderful success. The nobleman had invited some of his fine friends to view the furniture. They'd all been very impressed. Then the man had come up to Moshe to congratulate him.

"What is your name?" he asked, smiling.

"Mabovitch," Moshe had answered. "Moshe Mabovitch."

As Moshe stood there he saw the man's friendly smile fade. "Mabovitch?" he repeated, his eyes cold and sharp.

"Yes." Moshe drew himself up very straight. "Mabovitch."

"I'm afraid I was wrong," the man said, turning away. "This work isn't at all what I wanted."

"And he would not pay me," Moshe said. "But he did do me one big favor . . ."

"What?" Bluma whispered.

"He kept the furniture all the same."

Moshe lapsed into silence. As the weeks passed he was almost always silent. He worked—when there was work to be found. The rest of the time he just sat, doing nothing.

Then it was time for dinner one evening. "Eat," Bluma urged Moshe. "It will make you feel better."

But Moshe wasn't hungry. He began to talk instead—almost to himself at first.

"A privilege! I am told it is a privilege to be here in Kiev. Some privilege! Is it a privilege to eat potatoes without salt? Is it a privilege to drink water instead of wine? Is it a privilege to work and not be paid? I tell you, Bluma, such privileges I can do without!"

"I know, I know," she soothed. "But it could always be worse."

It could always be worse. This was something Bluma and Moshe often said to each other. Usually it helped. For no matter what troubles they had, they also had each other and their children.

But now Moshe didn't nod and smile as he usually did. He just went on talking.

"The rules, Bluma. I am so sick of them. What we can sell. What we can't sell. Where we can live. Where we can't live. Do you realize it's lucky we have only girls? They, at least, can grow up and get married. *That's* not against the rules. Not yet!

"But a son. What if we had a son? Just think of the things he couldn't be! He couldn't be a doctor or a lawyer or a teacher. He couldn't do anything that might let him earn a decent living. No, if he were lucky he might grow up and be a carpenter, like me—and watch his family go hungry, too!"

For the rest of the meal Moshe sat silent. But as Bluma began to clear off the table he spoke again. "I have made a decision. I am going to America."

America! Golda knew about America, for in the early 1900s many Jews were leaving Russia to settle there. Before long their letters started to come back, telling of the wonders of the place.

Almost every family on the street had a son or a nephew or a cousin who was already there. So every time one of these letters arrived there would be much calling back and forth. "It's from Hyam! In America!" the lucky receiver would cry. And everyone would gather to listen to the news—not only of Hyam—but also of America.

"But America . . ." Golda could tell Mama was scared. "It's so far away . . ."

"All the better," Moshe answered firmly. "Far away from Cossacks and soldiers and pogroms and policemen. Oh, I know that some of the stories of America aren't true. The Messiah hasn't come yet, not even there. And I don't believe that the streets will be paved with gold. But I do believe that those streets will be safe. I do believe that in America I will not have to take my cap off to every Cossack and rich man who passes by. I do believe that I can find work *and* be paid a fair wage!"

"When will you go?" Bluma asked.

"As soon as I can."

But was Papa going *alone?* Without the rest of them? Golda threw herself in his arms. "Take me with you, Papa!" she cried.

Moshe hugged his daughter tight. "I can't, Goldele," he explained gently. "Even after I sell everything—my tools and everything else—I'll be lucky to have enough for one ticket. But it is nothing to be upset about. In America I will get a good job. And I will save everything I can. Maybe I can make enough money to come back to Russia and live decently. But, if not, you will come to America. So don't worry. Before you know it we'll all be together again. Either here—or in America!"

3

"It's No Accident that You Were Named Golda"

Moshe Mabovitch left Kiev for America in the spring of 1903. Without his permit, his special dispensation to live outside the Pale, the rest of the family could no longer stay there either. So Bluma packed up the family's few possessions and returned to her hometown of Pinsk.

What a different place! Kiev had been a beautiful city of wide boulevards and magnificent mansions. In Pinsk most of the streets were narrow and twisting. Most of the buildings were tumbling down. Thirty thousand people lived crowded together in this hole-in-the-wall place. Most of them were Jewish. Most had to struggle hard just to exist.

Pinsk was famous for one thing, though. Mud. *Pinsker blotte* it was called. People said that in all of

Russia—no, in all of Eastern Europe—there was nowhere else where the mud was so thick and sticky.

Golda didn't care. Pinsk might be muddy and ugly and tumbledown, but from the first she was much happier there. For one thing she wasn't hungry. The food was plain. But there was enough of it. And that, as Golda realized very well by now, was what really mattered.

The reason for the food was simple. Bluma's father owned a tavern, so his business was serving meals. And when the Mabovitches returned to Pinsk, they moved in with him.

That tavern. Golda opened her mouth in an O of wonder at her first sight of it. For one thing it was so big—a full three stories tall. And it was made of brick. Golda had seen brick houses before, of course. But always from the road, just passing by. Now she was going to live in one!

The next few days Golda spent exploring. She started with the cellar. It was full of wonderful things to see and to smell. For it was there that Grandfather stored supplies for the tavern.

On shelves against the walls were stacks of plates and cups, containers of sugar and salt and coffee and tea, small sacks of rice and barley and all kinds of beans. What Golda liked best, though, were the rows of fruits and vegetables canned in glass, all glittering like jewels in the dim light.

On the floor nearby were big gunny sacks of potatoes and onions and apples. Then there were the barrels; one filled with mouth-puckering pickles, another with salt herring. And several others were brim full of schnapps, the fiery liquor that the customers loved to drink.

Every inch of that small cellar was used—even the floor itself. At the far end a deep ditch had been dug in the cool earth. Every winter Grandfather and his sons would go to the nearby river and hack out huge blocks of ice. They'd haul these blocks home and stack them in the ditch. Then they'd cover everything over with a thick blanket of straw. That was for insulation— it kept the ice from melting. Any food that might otherwise spoil could be stored for quite a while in Grandfather's "refrigerator."

Most of the first floor was taken up by one big room. This was the tavern itself. A long table stretched down the length of it. Here, every evening, customers gathered to eat and drink and have a good time.

Golda would stand behind the half-open door that led to the kitchen and watch everything that happened. She had never been to see a real play on a stage. She didn't even know such things existed. But all the same that's what she was watching from behind her door. The tavern room, with its smoky oil lamps casting warm yellow circles of light, was the stage itself. The customers were the actors. And Golda was a captivated audience of one.

On no two evenings was the action the same.

Often the room would ring with jokes and laughter and the sound of singing, for these men who came to the tavern worked hard all day. Now they wanted to relax and have a good time.

But sometimes things weren't so happy. Sometimes an argument would break out. Usually these arguments didn't come to much. But every once in a while the men would jump to their feet and begin to fight. Golda loved those moments of wild action. But they never lasted long enough, for Grandfather or one of her uncles would always come bustling forward to put an end to it.

Best of all Golda liked the evenings when the men drifted into serious discussions—wonderful rambling talks about good and evil, ethics, and all sorts of fine points of the Talmud—even if she couldn't understand a lot of what they were saying.

A stranger would have been surprised to come upon one of these discussions. For Grandfather's customers didn't look like learned men. They looked like what they were—storekeepers and laborers, blacksmiths and dairymen and garbage collectors.

According to the law, this was all they could be. Most of them could not attend high school, let alone college. But if these men could not go to Russian schools, they would go to schools of their own. If they could not get a proper education, they would get a makeshift one. But one way or another they *would* become educated. For according to Jewish tradition this was more important than anything else.

The tavern was the biggest room in the house. But Golda soon discovered that the heart of the house was the room behind. There in the kitchen Golda's mother and her aunts worked many hours a day to prepare the food that would be served in the evening. On a big table under the windows they snipped and sliced and chopped and pounded. On another table they kneaded dough for bread.

By mid-afternoon big pots of wonderful-smelling things would be simmering on top of the old black coal stove. These smells mingled mouth-wateringly with the yeasty smell of bread browning in the oven below.

How Golda loved those smells. But whenever she was near the stove she was always very careful, for between its curved iron legs one of the aunts kept a gaggle of geese.

The geese were fed choice scraps of garbage, for eventually, fat and juicy, they would become a central part of some happy holiday meal. Meanwhile, they were kept carefully penned, so they couldn't wander about the kitchen. But they were still a menace. For there was nothing to stop those mean-tempered birds from stretching out their long necks and taking a quick nip out of any bare leg that happened to wander too close—as Golda learned painfully more than once.

Golda had enough to eat, and a comfortable place to live. But most of all she was happy in Pinsk because of the people. In Kiev there had been only her immediate family. Here it was so different. For Grandfather had six children. Most of them were married and had children of their own. Many of these relatives worked in the tavern. They all lived close by. So Golda was surrounded by aunts and uncles and cousins of all ages.

This was especially important. All her life Golda was going to need other human beings close to her. She would never really be content alone. It was as natural as breathing for her to reach out for others. No wonder it was so easy to love her in return. Or that she was soon a special favorite in Grandfather's house.

This didn't mean that the relatives always approved of Golda. From their point of view she had one absolutely infuriating trait. There was no doubt about it, they all agreed. Golda was the most stubborn child they'd ever met.

It wasn't that Golda sulked or answered back. And she never screamed or created a fuss. It was just that when she felt she was right, she simply wouldn't obey—not even a direct order.

Naturally this upset most of the adults in her life. They simply weren't used to having their authority challenged—especially not by a girl. And such a *little* girl, too!

Years later people would talk about Golda's formidable will. This, they would say, was a big part of her amazing strength. But now the relatives called it stubbornness. And it sometimes made them very angry indeed.

They tried to reason with her. Then they shouted.

Sometimes they even spanked her. Nothing worked. When Golda had made up her mind, it stayed made up.

"There's a dybbuk in her!" one aunt exclaimed. *An evil and unruly spirit.*

Golda's mother agreed. "It's no accident you were named Golda!" she said more than once.

Bluma was angry whenever she said this. But Golda knew it was a compliment all the same. For Golda had been named for her great-grandmother. And Bobbe Golda—as everyone had called her—had been an extraordinary person.

Golda had never met Bobbe Golda, for the old woman had died when she was still a baby. But Golda felt as if she knew her very well. Bobbe Golda might be dead. But she was still a living legend in Pinsk.

Golda knew that Bobbe Golda had been very tall and thin, with smart brown eyes and deep lines of wisdom in her face. She had also been kind. But most of all she had been strong-willed. So strong-willed that inside and outside the family her smallest word very often became a command.

Bobbe Golda would probably have approved of what Golda did one April day soon after the family arrived in Pinsk. She might have approved—certainly no one else did.

As soon as Golda came downstairs that morning she knew something was wrong. All the relatives had gathered at the tavern. And they were terribly upset.

One of the aunts was weeping and wiping her face with her apron. Another was sitting in the corner wailing softly. Two of the uncles were pacing up and down the long tavern room, talking in fierce undertones and waving their arms in the air.

"What is it?" Golda asked. But her mother told her to go play outside. This was no business of hers.

Golda did go outside. But not to play. She went from group to group instead—for there were many people on the street that morning—and she listened to what they said.

Soon Golda's heart was hammering against her ribs, for she was hearing that scary word *pogrom* again. Only now the people weren't talking about an almost-pogrom—like the one in Kiev. They were talking about one that really had happened just a few days ago in the city of Kishinev.

It had all started quietly enough. Just a small mob of drunken peasants who'd broken into a Jewish store. They looted it and then burned it to the ground. But mobs have a way of growing. This one did. By mid-afternoon many stores and homes were burning.

With the coming of dark the mob stopped destroying houses and stores—and began destroying people instead. For three days and nights they rioted through the streets without opposition from the police.

"Only once did the police interfere," Golda heard a man say. "That was when they saw a group of Jews trying to defend themselves with the only weapons

4

"Cossacks!"

There were no pogroms in Pinsk. At least, not yet. But things were getting tenser all the time. One of the biggest reasons for this tension was the Cossacks. Just a few months ago a whole contingent had been sent to the town.

Cossacks! The very name was enough to frighten anyone. For they were wild men—wild and cruel—these horse-mounted soldiers of the czar.

One day Golda and a friend were playing in an alley near the tavern. They were sitting beside a mud puddle, pretending to make bread.

"The secret is kneading it enough," Golda said as she squeezed a ball of mud in her hands. "If you don't do that, do you know what will happen?"

Her friend shook her head.

"The bread will be heavy. It just won't rise right."

Golda patted the ball of mud into the shape of a loaf. "Then," she continued, "after you knead it, you—" She broke off, for she'd heard a faint *drum, drum, drumming* sound. It was growing louder. Suddenly Golda's eyes flared wide with panic. For she recognized it now. It was the sound of horses' hooves—pounding closer every moment!

Run! The word screamed through Golda's mind. But it never even formed in her throat. It was too late! Around the corner swept a group of Cossacks! The narrow alley seemed to explode with their shouts and curses.

The Cossacks saw the children, of course. But they didn't even try to stop. Down the alley they pounded, laughing like madmen. Closer and closer their horses galloped—straight for Golda and her friend!

The girls acted instinctively. They fell to the ground and froze with pure terror. That probably saved them. For at the very last moment the Cossacks jumped their horses, sailing through the air over the girls' heads. Golda stared straight up at the heavy metal hooves, flashing within an inch of her face.

Then, still roaring with laughter, the Cossacks landed and swept out of sight around a corner.

For the next few minutes the two girls just sat there in the mud, shaking. Finally Golda picked herself up and headed for home. She was splattered with mud from head to foot.

Usually mud didn't bother her. It was simply a fact of life in Pinsk. But somehow this mud was different. Somehow this mud made her feel strangely dirty—and yes, ashamed. So at home Golda slipped quickly out of her soiled dress and let it drop to the floor. Then she pumped a basin full of water and began to scrub herself all over.

Golda cried for a long time that night. But in a day or two she returned to normal. The Cossacks became just another memory she was working hard to forget.

Golda always woke on Friday morning with a special feeling of happiness—for at sundown on this day the Sabbath would begin.

There were all sorts of things you couldn't do on the Sabbath. You couldn't light a fire, so there was no way to heat food. You couldn't handle money. You couldn't carry burdens. You couldn't ride in a wagon or, God forbid, on a train. There were so many things you couldn't do on the Sabbath. But there was one thing you could always do—be happy.

But before sundown so many things had to be done! The whole house must be cleaned from top to bottom. The floors had to be swept and scrubbed. Even the woodwork had to be washed. And of course there were all sorts of special foods to be prepared.

Finally it was time! In a very few minutes the sun would set and the Sabbath would begin once more. Now, as the men left for a prayer service at the synagogue, the women and children of the house gathered around the long table in the tavern room for prayers of their own.

Soon the men returned from the synagogue. "Good Sabbath!" they called, as they struggled out of their coats and stamped the mud from their shoes.

"Good Sabbath!" everyone chorused in return.

Now they all gathered around the table for more prayers. Then Grandfather took a sip of wine and passed the goblet down the table. Finally it was time to sit down and enjoy the Sabbath feast.

And such a feast it was. There was always a big bowl of chicken soup with homemade noodles. There was roast chicken, too. There were carrots in a special sweet sauce, other vegetables, and noodles served in all sorts of ways—even as a sweet pudding with raisins for dessert. And everyone had a piece of *challeh,* of course—that braided white bread that was part of any special meal.

Laughter and jokes and interesting stories raced from one end of the table to the other. Golda and the other small children weren't expected to take much part in this conversation. But Golda didn't care. She had a perfectly grand time just listening.

Golda sat surrounded by uncles and aunts and cousins, for all the relatives came to Grandfather's for the Sabbath Eve meal. They weren't the only ones squeezed in around that long table, though. It was a Sabbath tradition to invite people who were too poor to make Sabbath for themselves, and strangers who happened to be passing through town. But nobody was really a stranger—not on Sabbath Eve.

Those were such happy evenings. But sometimes Golda's feeling of happiness would fade a little as she looked around the table. For no matter how crowded it was, one person was missing.

Papa wrote regularly from America, and his letters were always cheerful and full of bits of interesting information about that strange land. First he had settled in New York City. But it wasn't easy to find work. So the Hebrew Immigrant Aid Society had helped him move west to Milwaukee, Wisconsin. There he had found a job as a railroad carpenter. And soon he had joined a union—an organization of working men. This was something that could never have happened in Russia.

Only one thing was wrong. He was having a harder time saving money than he'd thought he would. In each letter he wrote, "Soon we will be together again." But more and more often lately Golda was asking herself, *how long is soon?* After all, they'd been in Pinsk for two years now. When would *her* very own family be complete again?

Bluma was not completely happy at Grandfather's either. She'd been married for many years, and most of those years she had run her own home. But at Grandfather's she was still a daughter, and not even the oldest one at that. Bluma became more and more determined to be the mistress of her own home again.

To do that, she would have to earn enough money for rent and food. Well, there was one thing everyone agreed she could do wonderfully well—bake bread and pastries and cakes.

Then that's what she'd do. She'd sell baked goods from door to door. Naturally, Grandfather was horrified. "A peddler? My daughter is going to become a common peddler?"

But Bluma would not be swayed. A few days later she announced that she had found a two-room house. True, there were a lot of things wrong with it. The rooms were small and dirty. The walls were caked with soot. But there was a big coal stove in the front room which would be perfect for baking bread. The stove would serve another purpose, she told her family cheerfully. It would also keep the little house warm on even the coldest winter night.

That big old coal stove soon became important to Golda, too. For tucked above it, next to the ceiling, was a wooden warming shelf. This shelf was Golda's special place.

It was where she went when she was lonely or unhappy. It was where she went when she wanted to think things through, or plan something important, or just daydream for a while. Above all, it was a place to go when she wanted to be alone.

For in this crowded house everything else had to be shared—even the bed she slept in had to be shared with Zipka. But the old warming shelf was hers alone.

One Saturday afternoon Golda was curled up on her shelf, daydreaming of this and that. Just at the moment when daydreams drift into real dreams, a gust of cold air filled the room. Golda opened her eyes and inched forward. She rubbed her eyes hard. Surely she was still dreaming! The room—which had been empty a moment before—was filling up with people. And not one of them was making a sound.

They were her sister Shaina's friends. And yes, here came Shaina. She shut the door and carefully locked it behind her.

"You stand guard at the window," she said quietly to a girl beside her. And then to the others, "Sit wherever you like."

The boys and girls settled themselves on the floor. Now Shaina moved over to the shelf by the stove. She was so close that Golda could have reached down and touched her. It would be fun to see her sister jump. But no. Maybe it would be better to wait. And listen.

Quickly Shaina filled the samovar with water. She carried it to the table and lit the little charcoal stove under it. "Remember," she said, "if anyone comes, we're having a Sabbath party."

Golda was puzzled. It was the Sabbath all right, but a party? This didn't look like any Sabbath tea party *she'd* ever seen. Where were all the happy people? Where was that special laughing-singing-joking party sound?

Now a tall boy stood up. Golda liked the way his

black hair fell so smoothly to his shoulders. His name was Shamai Korngold, she knew—and he was one of Shaina's closest friends.

But before he could speak, the girl at the window whirled around. "Shhh," she whispered fiercely. "Be quiet!"

"What is it?"

"It's Maxim!"

Maxim! Everyone held his breath, even Golda, hidden on her shelf. Maxim was a policeman—and all policemen were frightening. But he was the most frightening of them all. He was fat and red-faced, and he had small eyes like a pig. Those small pig eyes were sharp as needles. They seemed to be everywhere and to know everything that was going on.

"What's he doing?" someone whispered.

"Is he stopping?"

"Do you think he knows we're here?"

The girl didn't answer. She just stood by the window and watched. Then finally she gave a sigh of relief. "He only stopped to scratch himself . . ." Everyone laughed at that. "Now he's moving on. Yes, he's heading for the police station."

"That police station!" someone else whispered.

"I tell you, Shaina, it's not wise to meet here, so close to that place!"

"Yes! Whoever heard of holding an illegal meeting right down the street from a police station?"

Shaina shook her head. "No," she said firmly.

"That's what makes this place *really* safe. Who would think of looking for us here?"

Now Shamai held up his hand and the group fell silent. This Shamai Korngold must be the leader of whatever was going on, Golda thought. But what *was* going on?

She could hear what they were saying, all right. But she couldn't understand most of it. They talked about pamphlets . . . and a broken printing press . . . and a meeting that was going to be very dangerous . . . and something else even more dangerous that they planned to do in two weeks' time . . .

Suddenly all this talk of danger was too much for Golda. Suddenly she knew she had to stop them somehow. Now. "Shaina!" she blurted out.

Shaina gave a little cry and whirled around. Everyone else stifled sounds of shock and surprise.

The comments came thick and fast.

"My God! That's all we need—a kid!"

"And we thought this was a *secret* meeting!"

"Sure. It'll be all over Pinsk before sundown."

"No, it won't," Shaina said firmly. "My sister's no blabbermouth. I'll explain things to her—and she won't talk."

"I sure hope so. Anyway, it's time to leave," Shamai Korngold said. "We've been here long enough. Remember, next Saturday we meet at—" He looked at Golda. "Well, you know where."

Shaina unlocked the door and they all left. Now

she wheeled on her little sister. "Golda Mabovitch," she scolded. "What were you doing up there? Why didn't you *say* something when we came in?"

"I started to, but—"

"Oh, never mind! I suppose you heard everything?"

Golda nodded. "But I didn't understand a lot of it . . . exactly."

Shaina had to laugh. "People much older than you don't understand what's going on in Russia today."

Shaina held out her arms. "All right, Goldie. Come on down from there." She lifted her little sister to the ground.

"Now come over here. We've got to have a talk." Shaina led Golda over to the kitchen table. "Goldie, everything you heard today must be kept a secret."

"Why?"

"Well, you know how bad things are in Russia." Golda nodded.

"Well, we—the people you've just overheard— are trying to do something about it. We write pamphlets telling what is really going on, and then circulate them so they get into as many hands as possible. We help print a secret newspaper. Sometimes we organize protest meetings. That's very dangerous. Although not as dangerous as the espionage . . ."

"Es-pionage?"

"Never mind," Shaina said hastily. "That's something you *don't* have to understand."

Golda was confused. "But why, Shaina? Why are you doing all these dangerous things?"

"Because," Shaina answered, "we—and all the other underground groups in Russia—are trying to overthrow the government of the czar."

"The *czar!*" Golda gasped.

"Yes. And we have nothing. No guns, no money, no power. Nothing! But I tell you this, Golda. We will win all the same!"

Golda felt a glow of pure pride as she gazed at her sister. How beautiful Shaina looked—and how fierce!

Golda was still confused about a lot of what Shaina was saying. But in some almost wordless way she did understand that it wasn't enough just to believe in something. A person had to be prepared to struggle for that belief, too. "I must have begun, when I was about six or seven," Golda wrote many years later, "to grasp the philosophy that underlay everything that Shaina did. That there is only one way to do anything. The right way."

"But meanwhile, Goldie," Shaina continued, "if the czar's police or the Cossacks find out what we're doing, do you know what will happen?"

Golda shook her head.

"We will be arrested."

Wordlessly, Golda pointed down the street.

Shaina nodded. "Yes, the police station. We'll be

questioned for hours. If we don't talk, the police will probably whip us—with ropes and straps and metal rods.''

Golda shuddered.

"Oh, Goldie!" Shaina pulled Golda close. "I don't want to scare you. But I have to make you understand how important it is to keep absolutely quiet about what you've heard today. For sometimes the police do worse than just beat people. Sometimes they send their prisoners to Siberia. And most people never come back from there.''

Golda gulped. "Shaina, I promise. I'll never say *anything*. Never!''

"I know you won't, Goldie," Shaina said gently. "Oh, and one thing more. Don't tell Mama, either. She would only worry.''

In the next few months things grew even tenser in Pinsk. An extra detachment of Cossacks was sent to the city. And the police seemed to be everywhere. People weren't even safe in their beds, for it was becoming a common practice to search a suspect's home late at night.

The first warning would be a sudden banging on the door. Sometimes, after tearing the house apart, the police would just make a few threats and leave. But more and more often—whether they found anything or not—they were arresting people, most of them teenage boys and girls like Shaina.

The Christians of Pinsk were becoming more hostile, too. Many were ignorant peasants, and they found it increasingly easy to believe the czar's anti-Jewish propaganda.

One day Golda and a friend were standing in the front yard. Suddenly Golda heard a song. She looked up to see a drunken peasant wandering down the street toward them, singing cheerfully.

But just as he reached them the peasant's mood took a drunken shift. His grin turned to a fierce scowl. Suddenly he reached out and grabbed the two girls. Then he banged their heads together.

"That's what we'll do with all the Jews," he shouted. "And then we'll be through with them!"

His good humor suddenly restored, he weaved off down the street again, roaring with laughter.

Golda didn't cry. She was too furious for that. She was only seven years old, but she was coming dangerously close to being filled with hate.

A few hours later Shaina came home to find her sitting at the kitchen table. For a few minutes Shaina puttered around, talking of this and that. But Golda, usually so cheerful and chatty, just sat there, staring straight ahead.

Shaina sat down opposite her and took one of her hands. "What's wrong, Goldie?"

Finally Golda spoke. "Why can't they leave us alone?" she asked between clenched teeth.

"Who?"

"Them!" Golda snatched her hand away and pounded it against the table. *"Peasants! Christians!"*

"Oh," Shaina said. It took a while, but finally

39

she got the whole story out of Golda. Then she nodded.

"Look, Goldie, it was terrible, what happened. But you've got to understand that—"

"I *hate* them!" Golda muttered.

"No, you mustn't do that. Look, Golda, you know the risks my friends and I are taking. Well, we're doing that to make life in Russia better for *everybody*. Not just for Jews. For Christians, too."

"Why?" Golda's voice was almost a wail. "Why do you care about *them*? They don't care about us!"

"It's true what you say. There are many ignorant people in Russia who believe the czar's propaganda, and the Church's. But there are many others who do not hate. Why, all over Russia there are Christian groups fighting just as hard as we are."

Golda remained unconvinced.

Shaina sat still for a few moments. She wanted to gather just the right words for what she had to say next. "Goldie, we believe it's wrong for them to hate us just because we're Jews. But isn't that what you're beginning to do—in reverse?"

For a minute or two Golda continued to stare down at the table. Then slowly she began to relax. When she looked up, Shaina breathed a sigh of relief. For Golda's eyes were clear and gentle once more.

Shaina had sworn Golda to secrecy. And Golda was true to her promise. But rumors have a way of spreading in a small town like Pinsk. Before long Bluma Mabovitch knew exactly what her oldest daughter was doing. And she didn't like it at all.

First she tried to reason with Shaina. But Shaina refused to listen. So before long Bluma stopped being reasonable and began to issue orders. Shaina paid no attention to this either. Finally Bluma began to yell.

"You'll land in jail!"

"I don't matter!" Shaina yelled right back.

"Then think of us—your family!"

"Mama, don't you understand? What I'm doing is important!"

"Staying alive is important, too!"

Poor Golda. She listened to these arguments—and felt trapped between these two people she loved so much. On the one hand, she thought what Shaina was doing was absolutely wonderful. But on the other hand, Golda could also understand how her mother felt.

It wasn't easy to watch Shaina slip out of the house after supper and know she might not return until almost dawn. And to wonder what terrible risks she was taking in those dark hours in between.

Sometimes, in the middle of the night, the silence would be ripped apart by high knife-sharp screams of pain. Then Golda knew that Maxim and his friends were busy "questioning" someone in the police station down the road.

It hadn't been Shaina—so far. But always the next

morning there would be a big fight. More and more often those fights would end with Mama in tears.

"I can't bear any more! Every time I hear screaming coming from there I know it's you!" she would sob. "Each time it's you! I ask you, Shaina, how many times must I die of fright?"

Then one morning Shaina came home with her skirt ripped and dirt all over her face. She wouldn't explain what had happened. "It would just worry you," she said.

But Bluma soon found out. The police had raided a house where Shaina and her friends were meeting. Some of the others had been arrested. But Shaina had managed to escape by crawling through a second-story window and shinnying down a drainpipe.

This time Bluma didn't waste time arguing. She didn't say anything at all. She just sat down and wrote to Moshe in America.

"It doesn't matter if you've saved enough money or not," she wrote. "Believe me, we must come. *Now!*"

5

"Mil-wauuu-keeeeee!"

That trip from Russia to America was so long—and
sometimes so boring. There would be much that Golda
would soon forget. But other things she would remember all her life—like parts of a dream.

First was the train station in Pinsk. Grandfather
and all the aunts and uncles and cousins were gathered
around. Some of the aunts were crying. But it was
Grandfather who was really upset. He was stamping up
and down the platform, his voice only a little lower
than a bellow.

"In America, there are so many tempting things,
so many new ways," he was shouting. "They will dis-
tract you! You will forget the old customs!"

"No, no," Bluma promised. "You must not
worry, Father. Wherever we are we will keep the old
ways. We will keep a kosher home. I promise."

And then they were on the train—and Pinsk was gone, gone forever.

Then it was much later, and the train had stopped. As they all climbed down, an old woman appeared out of the shadows. "Mrs. Mabovitch?" she whispered.

"Yes," Bluma answered.

The old woman motioned them to follow her. She led them through the streets of a small town. Finally they came to a primitive hut on the edge of a woods.

Without speaking, the woman gave them tea and hunks of black Russian bread. The place was bare of furniture, except for some pallets stuffed with straw in the corner, so they sat on the floor to eat. Whenever they talked they kept their voices very low.

All this secrecy was very necessary. Proper passports cost a lot of money, and Moshe Mabovitch had not been able to send enough to buy them. So his wife and daughters were leaving the country illegally—as many had been forced to do before.

This old woman was part of a group of people paid to sneak them across the border into Poland. From there on things might continue to be uncomfortable, but they would never be as dangerous again.

Now a man came into the hut. His greasy hair hung down over his eyes, but Golda could see that he was scowling fiercely. He and Bluma fell into a conversation so low that Golda could only catch bits of it. What she did understand wasn't comforting.

The Mabovitches were supposed to cross the border by train. But the man said the authorities had been alerted, so that way was too dangerous. They would have to go by wagon through the woods instead.

There was something about the way the man looked . . . Something about his tone of voice . . . Golda did not believe him. It was plain that Bluma didn't either.

"You're trying to cheat me," she said angrily. "I've already given you people the money for the train. Now you're trying to pocket some of it!"

"Be quiet!" the man ordered. "It's dangerous to talk so loud."

"I'll tell you what is dangerous," Bluma said. "A wagon! Going through the woods is more dangerous! And I will not do it. I'll go back to Pinsk instead, and tell everyone what you have done. No one will ever trust you again."

The man had met his match in Bluma. The next morning the Mabovitches crossed the border by train. But even that was dangerous. At the border everyone's passport was checked. Of course Bluma and the girls had none of their own, so they'd been supplied with other people's. When they got to a safe place they were supposed to mail them back.

It was good that no one looked at those passports too closely. Forty-year-old Bluma was carrying the passport of a twenty-year-old. Seventeen-year-old Shaina loosened her hair and tried to look twelve. It was lucky that Golda was small for her age, for her passport announced she was five! Four-year-old Zipka had a different problem. She had to cross with a total stranger. "Remember to call her Mama!" Bluma ordered.

After that things got pretty jumbled in Golda's memory. Somewhere in Poland their luggage had been stolen . . . They slept for two nights in a cold, drafty barn . . . Sometimes they walked, and sometimes they rode in the backs of bouncing wagons . . . Then there was another train . . . And finally, after almost two weeks, they reached the Belgian port city of Antwerp.

What a relief that was! They were taken to a refugee center where they had their first hot baths since leaving Pinsk. How good that water felt. And the hot meal that followed it.

By this time their clothes were practically in rags. But clever Bluma had sewn a few coins in the hem of her skirt—just in case. Now she removed them and brought each of the girls a new set of clothes. They would have to wear them every day, and wash them out at night. "Take good care of them," Bluma warned. "They are all you will have until we get to Milwaukee."

Milwaukee! Golda was beginning to wonder if such a place really existed.

A few days later, along with hundreds of other refugees, the Mabovitches boarded a ship for America. The ship was small and the seas were rough during that two-week period in the spring of 1906. Many people spent the whole time moaning and groaning with seasickness.

But not Golda. She loved to stand on deck, gripping the vibrating rail, and feel the ship heaving and tossing beneath her feet. She loved the way the wind whipped through her hair as she stared across the empty ocean toward America.

The trip so far had only confused poor Zipka. So Golda often would sit with her little sister and tell her stories about the wonderful things to come. Glory Stories about America.

Zipka's favorite was about the house they would live in. "Tell me what it will look like, Goldie," she begged.

"Oh, not again!"

But then Zipka's face would begin to crumple. So Golda would start. "In Milwaukee, America, our house will not be like the one in Pinsk. It won't be small and dirty. It will be big and painted white, with—"

"With green shutters," Zipka breathed.

"Yes," Golda agreed. "With bright green shutters. Or maybe bright red, what do you think?"

Zipka shook her head.

"All right, green. And there will be a big yard all around the house—"

"With grass everywhere," Zipka added.

"Yes. And around the yard will be a fence—"

Zipka clapped her hands. "With roses climbing all over it!"

And so the Glory Story would go on and on.

When the ship docked there was one last train ride

through strange fields and forests and towns. Then at last . . .

"Mil-wauuu-keeeeee!" the conductor sang out. "All out for Milwaukee!" Journey's end at last!

Golda and the others stumbled off the train. And there, striding down the platform toward them, was Papa!

Or was it? Golda recognized him . . . and yet she didn't. He looked so *different*. What was it? Suddenly Golda knew. He'd shaved off his beard, his wonderful curly black beard!

"In America this is the way men look," he explained later.

But Golda wasn't sure she liked it. Not at all. It made her feel very shy.

Now Papa and Mama were hugging each other very hard. Papa gave Shaina a kiss, too. Then he looked down at Golda and smiled. "Well, Goldie, don't I get a kiss after all this time?"

As he spoke the strange feeling faded. Warm memories came rushing back. Even Zipka crept out from behind Mama's skirts, where she'd been hiding.

"Come, let's go home," Papa said. He held out one hand to Golda and the other to Zipka. As the family walked down the platform they all began to talk at once. And suddenly Golda knew that everything was going to be all right.

Moshe led them to an automobile standing outside

the station. Golda's eyes popped open. She'd seen automobiles before. But she'd never *ridden* in one.

"Is this *ours?*" Zipka's voice was full of wonder.

"No," Moshe laughed. "I hired it. Not only that, I hired it by the hour, so hurry up and hop in!"

The auto began to move. Golda turned and twisted in her seat, for there was so much to see everywhere! The streets were wide—as wide as the biggest boulevard at home. They were shaded by beautiful kinds of trees that Golda had never seen before. The houses, to a little girl fresh from Pinsk, looked big and beautiful, too.

"See, Zip!" she whispered. "White houses!"

That was one trip that was over too soon. Only a few minutes later Moshe came to a stop before a very large stone house.

"Is all of *this* ours?" Zipka asked.

"No, Zip," Moshe told her, smiling. "This is an apartment house. Many families live here. Come." He led them upstairs and into a big airy apartment.

"Is all of this ours?" Zipka asked again.

Now Moshe did not smile at all.

"Well, no. You see, I wasn't given much time."

Bluma began to frown.

Moshe led them down a long dark hall and opened still another door. A door leading to a single room. "It won't be for long," Moshe said.

Golda refused to look at Zipka. But she could feel her little sister's eyes boring into the back of her head.

And why not? Hadn't she told Zip all those Glory Stories? How they were going to live in a big white house with bright green shutters . . . . Now here they were, all five of them, crowded together into one room.

"Back home we had two rooms." Zipka's voice was full of accusation.

"Well, this is your home now!" Moshe's voice was just as sharp. Then it softened. "But don't worry, little Zipka. We'll find something better soon. I promise."

Golda heard Mama sigh. She was only eight years old, but she knew just what that sigh meant. Papa was wonderful, of course. He was learned and gentle. He told all sorts of funny stories and jokes. And he always had room in his heart for the troubles of other people. But Golda also knew that if you wanted something done—done right and done quickly—it was better for Mama to do it. Mama made things happen. With Papa it was just the other way around. Somehow things just seemed to happen to him.

But that was the low point of the day. For just then Mrs. Badner, the lady who rented Moshe his room, came bustling in. Golda liked her right away. "Welcome," she said. "Welcome to America!"

Before anyone could answer she continued, "Is everything all right? I wanted to give you a few minutes to settle in. But dinner will be ready soon."

"Oh, we couldn't intrude on—" Bluma began.

"Intrude!" Mrs. Badner held up her hands in mock horror. "Such a word! When I've been looking forward to your arrival so! Why, I've been cooking for days—just for you!"

Bluma looked down at her clothes. "I'm sorry we look like such beggars, but our luggage was—"

Mrs. Badner threw up her hands again. "Stop, stop," she cried cheerfully. "Do you think I don't remember? When it's only three years since I got here from Poland myself? But come. The best thing about dirt is how easily it washes off. I've got some hot water heating in the kitchen now. And after you wash, maybe you would all like a nice glass of hot tea."

Mrs. Badner waggled her finger playfully. "But no food. That will come later. I wouldn't want you to ruin your appetites so close to my meal." Then, like a mother hen, she gathered Bluma and the girls together, and herded them down a hall toward the kitchen.

Mrs. Badner had not exaggerated. That first meal in Milwaukee was a real feast. There was gefilte fish— "Just to make you feel at home," Mrs. Badner said. And a big tureen full of savory spinach soup. There were platters of roast meat and a roast chicken, too.

By the time the meal was over Golda wasn't sure she could find room for her piece of flaky apple strudel. But somehow she managed.

That night Golda lay in bed, too happy to sleep. What if things weren't just as she'd imagined them? she thought. What if they weren't anything like the

Glory Stories she'd told Zipka? What did all that matter? No, what really mattered was that she could reach out and touch each and every person she loved best in the world. The Mabovitches were a family again!

Early the next morning Bluma set out to find a place to live. It wouldn't be easy, Mrs. Badner told her, for it was 1906 and times were hard in Milwaukee. And of course the Mabovitches had almost no money.

But Bluma was Bluma, and once more she accomplished what she set out to do. Every morning she went out, and a few days later she came back, beaming. "Some people might not like it," she said. "But I think it's perfect for us."

The rest of the family agreed when they saw it. The Mabovitches knew from the first that they were going to be happy in that small two-story house on the corner of 6th and Walnut streets.

The house was shabby and the yard full of weeds. "But houses can be painted. Weeds can be pulled," Bluma said cheerfully, as she started to lead them on a tour of inspection.

Most of the rooms were small and dark, but everyone marveled at how many there were. On the ground floor there was a big front room. Behind this was a small kitchen, and off the kitchen an even smaller room with no windows.

"But who needs windows at night?" Bluma asked. "They only let in cold air. What do you think, Moshe, wouldn't this make a good bedroom for us?"

Upstairs there was a living room with a big pot-bellied stove, and two more bedrooms. Golda would have to share one of those rooms. But she didn't mind. She'd been sleeping with Zipka ever since her little sister had been a baby. Probably she would find it lonely to sleep any other way.

"Well," Bluma said, as she led them downstairs again. "What do you think?"

Think! Everyone *knew*. Compared to Pinsk this place was a palace! The next hour flew as they began to explore, discovering one marvel after another. Shaina was particularly intrigued with the built-in running water. In Pinsk if you wanted water you had to go outside and pump it from a well. This was never easy, for the old pump was cranky and stiff with age. In the winter everything was likely to freeze—the water, the handle, and the person trying to pump. But here all you had to do was turn a knob and water came gushing out.

Golda loved the gaslights. They were so much brighter and cleaner than the old oil lamps back home. Besides, they didn't smell.

But it was Zipka who discovered the most wonderful thing of all. She had been out in the backyard looking over the outhouse. Now she came tearing inside again. "It flushes!" she yelled. "You just pull a chain and the water washes everything away!"

"Really, Zipka!" Shaina's voice was severe. "People don't talk about such things."

But for days the whole family—including

Shaina—would give that chain an extra pull, just to see the water gurgling down the drain.

Bluma had one more surprise for her family. She was a very energetic and independent woman. And her one effort at earning money in Pinsk had pleased her very much. Now she led everyone back to the big room at the front of the house.

"Look," she said, sweeping her arm around. "What does it look like? I mean, with those big windows and all?"

"A store!" she answered herself triumphantly. "And that's what it will be. As soon as we are settled I'm going to open a grocery store! And I'll sell fruit and vegetables and milk and butter . . ."

"And pickles, too, Mama?" Zipka asked.

"Yes," Bluma laughed. "Pickles, too."

For the next few days everyone was very busy. Bluma and the girls scrubbed and polished everything in sight. Then they tackled the cupboards and closets. Moshe did his share, too. He made shelves and a long table for the store.

"But that is all I will do," he announced as he finished. "If you are so determined to have a store, Bluma, you will have to run it yourself. I am a carpenter. A union man! Not a grocery clerk!"

"Mama, can I go for a walk?" Golda asked one morning soon after they had moved in.

"Why not?" Bluma answered. "But come back soon. There's still so much to do."

Off Golda went. Right next door she found what looked like a shop. There was even some strange-looking gold lettering on the big glass window in front. Golda couldn't read it, of course. So she went closer and peered through the window.

What she saw made her blink with surprise. Standing behind a counter piled high with towels and sheets was a little man. He had slanted eyes and he wore his shiny black hair in a braid down his back! He bowed politely. So Golda bowed back. She had met her first man from China.

Golda wanted to go inside and talk to him. But she felt a little shy, so she continued on down 6th Street. She'd already noticed that the street was paved. So she figured it must be an important one—in Pinsk only the really important streets had been paved.

But now Golda turned a corner, and the next street was paved too. And the next. And the next. Finally she realized that *all* the streets here were paved. For a moment Golda stood very still. And something that had been tense and tight within her relaxed. For the first time she really believed that the mud of Pinsk—and all it stood for—was a thing of the past.

Golda had a great deal of fun that summer. But she also set herself a very important task. She could already speak Yiddish and Russian and a smattering of Hebrew. But soon fall would be here and she'd be going to school. More than anything Golda wanted to be able to speak English by then.

It wasn't easy to practice at home, for her family and most of the neighbors spoke Yiddish. Many of them saw no need to learn what they considered to be a foreign language.

The Chinese next door was an exception. He didn't speak Yiddish at all. To be honest, he didn't speak English very well either. But still, before that first summer was over, he and Golda had become good friends.

He didn't have many friends. Most of the people in the neighborhood avoided him because to them he looked so strange. One day Golda saw a group of children sneak up to the open door of his laundry shop and yell inside, "Chinky-chinky-Chinaman!" and then race away, laughing wildly.

Golda watched as he came to the door and stood looking out. Perhaps it was because she remembered a peasant knocking two little girls' heads together and then roaring with laughter . . . Perhaps it was because she saw the hurt in his eyes before he turned away— but from then on Golda went out of her way to be nice to the man.

She ran errands for him whenever she could. And they spent as much time as they could spare in the steamy shop talking, less and less haltingly, in the only language they had in common—English.

Moshe had taken Golda and Zipka aside soon after they arrived in Milwaukee. "This is a safe town," he said. "But it's also pretty big. So it's possible you might get lost. If that happens, don't worry. Just look around for a policeman. Tell him your address and he will see that you get home safe and sound.''

A *what?* Golda and Zipka looked at each other, astonished. Then they looked at Papa. He was serious! He wasn't joking! But a *policeman?* They looked at each other again. They didn't say anything—then or later—but they both knew they would do nothing of the kind.

Then it was September. Tomorrow the Mabovitches would celebrate their first American holiday. Labor Day had been set aside to honor all people who worked with their hands.

The highlight of the day would be a grand parade down the main street of Milwaukee. Golda and the others could talk of little else for weeks. For Papa, along with the other members of his carpenters' union, was going to be marching in that parade!

Finally the day arrived. The sun was shining brightly and there was a slight nip in the air. ''A perfect day for a parade,'' Moshe said. ''Not too hot and not too cold.''

Right after breakfast he put on his perfectly pressed suit and his newly shined shoes. He was holding a new straw hat in his hand. ''How do I look?'' he asked.

''Papa, Papa!'' Golda and Zipka cried, dancing around him. ''You look *grand!*''

Moshe gave each of them a hug. "Remember, Bluma," he said as he left to join the other members of his union, "leave enough time so you can get a good spot to see everything. I hear the crowds are really big."

"Leave the dishes to soak in the sink," Bluma told the girls. "We'll do them later." So Golda and her sisters raced upstairs to put on their best dresses—so stiffly starched they almost stood by themselves. Next they slipped on their freshly polished shoes. Finally each of them tied a big ribbon in her hair.

"Today is not a day to walk," Bluma announced as they were leaving the house. "Today we will take a streetcar!"

As they neared the parade route they could see all sorts of people streaming downtown. But they were lucky. They found a place right by the curb. Even little Zipka would be able to see everything that went on.

Soon, with the crash of cymbals and the boom of big bass drums, the parade began. Group after group of workers marched by, each carrying a banner to identify itself. In between were brass marching bands—every band member playing as loudly as possible.

And then there were the floats. One was a huge figure of the Statue of Liberty, carrying a real lighted torch in her upraised hand. Others showed different scenes from the American labor movement. Golda's favorite was a group of people wrapped in chains. Some were completely bowed down by them. Others were in the process of rising and casting them off. Along the side of the float was a sign, saying: "Don't be Chained. Join a Union and Free Yourself Too!" And everything, even the sign, was made of flowers!

Suddenly Golda saw her father. "Papa! Papa!" she and Zipka jumped up and down and screamed. He must have heard them for he smiled just a little. But he never turned his head as he marched proudly by.

Oh! What a glorious day! Golda felt like hugging herself for the pure joy of it. Then it happened. Policemen on horses had been stationed along the street to help control the happy crowds. One happened to be right in front of the Mabovitches.

Now a small boy darted out into the street. With a gleeful yell he threw a smoking firecracker into the air. It fell and went off with a terrific bang! right under the police horse's front hooves.

This was too much for even a well-trained horse. It reared high in the air—right over Zipka. "Cossacks!" she screamed, and fell to the ground in a dead faint.

By afternoon Zipka was running a high fever. The doctor was called and examined her carefully. "It's nothing to worry about," he said. "She's suffered a bad shock. Keep her warm and quiet. And don't worry. She'll be fine in a few days."

But Moshe and Bluma did worry. After everyone else was asleep that night they sat in the kitchen and talked.

"She seemed so happy this summer," Bluma said. "I hoped she'd forgotten the Cossacks—and everything else . . ."

"Yes," Moshe agreed. "I did, too. But perhaps we hoped for too much. Perhaps there are certain memories that never fade—not completely."

Bluma nodded sadly. For a few moments they sat there, silent and sad with their thoughts.

Then Moshe spoke again. "But just think of all the *new* memories she has already made this summer. Good memories of America."

6

"I Pledge Allegiance to the Flag..."

As soon as Golda woke up she knew, *something wonderful is going to happen today*. But what? The sun was streaming in through the window by her bed. It wasn't that. And today wasn't a holiday. It was . . . Suddenly Golda's eyes popped open. Now she remembered! Today was the first day of school!

Golda had gone to school in Russia—a little. But the teacher had been a sleepy old rabbi who'd only taught her and the other girls in her class a little Hebrew and a smattering of Jewish history. And even that cost money. So Golda had not gone often.

But here in America it was different. Here both boys *and* girls were expected to attend a real school. Not just for a few hours a week either. Here all children under the age of fourteen were expected to go to school from nine in the morning to three in the afternoon, five days a week, for almost ten months a year. It wasn't just expected. It was the law!

Now Golda turned toward her little sister who was still sound asleep on the other side on the bed. "Zip! Wake up! And hurry! We've got to get ready for school!"

"Mmmmmmmmhf!" Zipka muttered. "I'm not going." Then she burrowed more deeply under the covers. Zipka knew from her neighborhood friends that in America children didn't have to start school until they were five. And she was only four.

"So why do *I* have to go?" she'd asked her mother for the umpteenth time only yesterday.

"Look, Zip!" Bluma exclaimed. "I'll tell you once more—and then that's it! I wish you could stay home with me. But you can't. Shaina is working in that factory. Golda will be in school most of the day. And I'll be too busy with the store to look after you. So you've just got to go."

"But . . ."

"No more buts," Mama said firmly. "Besides, you're making a mountain out of a molehill. Once you're there you'll probably like it a lot."

That's what everyone said. Zipka was not nearly so sure. But since she had no real choice she got dressed—slowly—and went downstairs to breakfast with Golda. Mama handed them both brown paper sacks. "Don't lose them," she warned. "Or you won't have any lunch."

Right after breakfast the sisters started out for school. Once more Zipka tried to hang back. "Hurry up, Zip!" Golda scolded again and again. "One thing we aren't going to be is late for school. Not on the first day!"

A few minutes later they were standing in front of the sprawling three-story red brick building.

"It's so big," Zipka whispered.

"Yes," Golda answered happily.

The yard in front was crowded with boys and girls, all yelling and dashing about. Some were only a little bigger than Zipka. Others towered over Golda.

What a crowd—and what a racket, too! For a moment even Golda hesitated. But then one of the big boys began to shout. "New pupils over here! Everyone else go to last year's rooms—you'll be assigned from there."

Golda and Zipka joined the long line that was forming in front of the boy. A few minutes later he led them into the school and down a long corridor. Finally the line stopped in front of a door with gilt lettering on it.

"What's going on?" Golda asked a girl in front of her.

"All new kids have to talk to the principal," the girl explained. "You know, you give him your name and stuff like that. Then he tells you what class you're going to be in."

Slowly the line inched forward until Golda and

Zipka were standing before a tall, kind-looking man. This was the principal, Mr. Finn.

"What's your name?" he asked.

"Golda," she replied.

"Hummmmm . . ." He hesitated. "Yes, it will do. And what's your last name?"

"Mabovitch."

Mr. Finn scanned the sheaf of papers he was holding in his hand. "Yes, here you are." He made a check by her name.

"Golda," he continued, "I see that you've never really been to school before. So you *should* be in the first grade. But since you're eight years old I think we'll put you in the second, instead. That means you must apply yourself diligently. Do you under-stand?"

Dil-igent-ly? Golda's English was still a little shaky. But she certainly understood the important part of what he was saying.

"Yes, sir!" she answered happily. "I will!"

Now Mr. Finn turned toward Zipka, who was clinging tightly to Golda's hand. "I assume you are a Mabovitch, too," he said, smiling. "What's your first name?"

Zipka, whose English was not nearly as good as her big sister's, turned worried eyes toward Golda. "He wants to know your name," Golda told her in Yiddish.

Zipka looked up at the tall man shyly. "Zipka," she whispered.

"Zipka?" Mr. Finn frowned. "What kind of a name is that?"

"Her real name is Zipporah," Golda volunteered. "We just call her Zipka."

But obviously this didn't sound any better to Mr. Finn's Irish ear. "Won't do . . ." he murmured. "Won't do at all . . . You are in America now, so you should have an American name. Yes, from now on your name will be . . . Clara!"

Clara Mabovitch he wrote down in his records. And a few minutes later a thoroughly confused Zipka—or Clara, as she would be called from then on outside the family—was led down the hall toward the kindergarten room.

When Golda got to her class a number of boys and girls were milling around the room. "Just take any seat, any seat at all," a pretty young woman called out from the front of the room. "I'll straighten you all out in a moment."

Golda took the first empty seat she saw. It happened to be next to a tall girl with bright brown eyes. "My name's Golda," Golda whispered. "Golda Mabovitch."

"Mine's Regina," the girl answered. "Regina Hamburger."

Regina Hamburger, Golda repeated to herself. Somehow she knew that this girl was going to be a very special friend. But they had no more time to talk then. The teacher was rapping on her desk.

"As most of you know," she announced when the class grew quiet, "the first thing we do every day is stand and say the Pledge of Allegiance to the Flag. All right, class, please rise."

"I pledge allegiance to the flag of the United States of America," she began—and most of the students joined in. Golda, of course, didn't know the words, so she just listened. But it only took her a few days to master them; then she spoke them proudly.

After a little while, though, she began to realize that many of the other boys and girls were just sliding through the words, blurring them into one long nonsense sound. This was something Golda could never understand. She was always careful to say each and every word as clearly and distinctly as she could.

For they meant a great deal to a little girl so recently arrived from Russia. The final words especially. *With liberty and justice for all*. That always gave Golda a special shiver of pleasure. *With liberty*—to do what you wanted and not be afraid. *And justice*—instead of secret searches and terrifying screams in the night. *For all*—not just for the rich and powerful, not just for the privileged few, but for all!

So school began for Golda. From the beginning it was everything she had hoped it would be. She adored her teacher. Before long she had all sorts of friends. But best of all were the lessons. For the first time in her life Golda was learning in an organized way. She loved every minute of it.

Golda's favorite subject was history—especially stories of early times in America. She learned about the Indians and the Pilgrims and the first Thanksgiving dinner. But most of all she liked to hear about the thirteen original colonies and how they had struggled to free themselves from the domination of England.

One day the teacher held up a strange-looking piece of paper. "This is a copy of the Declaration of Independence," she said. This was the document, she continued, that the Founding Fathers had written to explain why they were willing even to fight a bloody war to gain the freedom they craved so much.

Now she started to read: "When in the Course of Human Events, it becomes necessary for one People to dissolve the Political Bands which have connected them with another, and to assume among the Powers of the Earth, the separate and equal Station to which the Laws of Nature and of Nature's God entitle them . . ."

Such words! They filled Golda with a sense of awe. How much greater that feeling of awe would have been if she could have seen into the future. If she could have known that on a warm May day in the year 1948 she too would sign her name to a declaration much like this—and by so doing help found the new country of Israel.

Winter came, and then spring. Almost too soon Golda's first year of school was over. In the fall of

1907 another year began. One late fall day Regina raced up to Golda on the playground.

"Where have you been?" she said breathlessly. "I've been waiting for you! Here! Look at these!" She waved two pieces of brightly colored cardboard under Golda's nose.

"What are they?" Golda asked.

"Tickets!" Regina answered, her eyes dancing with excitement. "Tickets to a real live play!"

Golda was still puzzled. "Where'd you get them?"

"Oh, someone gave them to my parents. But they can't go. Oh, Goldie, let's go ourselves!"

"When are they for?"

"Well," Regina answered slowly. "That's the only trouble. They're for tomorrow afternoon."

"But that's a school day!"

"I know," Regina said. "But the play will only be here for one day."

Golda frowned. The thought of cutting school had never crossed her mind before. But to see a play . . . With real live actors . . . She'd never been to a play before. When would she get the chance again? After a moment, her eyes began to dance too.

Next morning the girls went to school as usual. But after lunch they headed downtown. By the time they arrived at the theater they were in a high state of nerves. What would their teacher say when she discovered that their seats were empty? What would their *mothers* say? And what if the people at the theater didn't let in girls their age? What if there was some sort of rule saying they had to be accompanied by adults?

But the usher didn't even give them a glance as he took their tickets. "Top balcony," he said, yawning. "Stairs over there."

Golda and Regina climbed and climbed until there were no more stairs. Then another usher showed them to their seats. What a place! Golda didn't know where to look first. Her seat was covered with red velvet plush. The curtain across the stage below was also made of red velvet. The creamy white walls were decorated with clusters of gold flowers and curling gold vines. Hanging from the ceiling were many crystal chandeliers, their cut-glass prisms throwing off bright glitters of light.

Now the audience fell silent as those chandeliers began to dim. There was one magic moment of total dark. Then the curtain began to rise.

The play was *Uncle Tom's Cabin,* a very famous play about the days of slavery in the United States. The hero was Uncle Tom, of course—a kind and religious and obedient slave. At first the play was happy, for his master was a good man. But then his master fell deeply into debt. To pay off this debt he would have to sell some of his most valuable possessions. One of these possessions was Tom.

A slave trader came to the house and the deal was

soon made. The very next morning Tom was torn away from his family and sold—auctioned off to the highest bidder, like a horse or a sheep or a cow. He was sold several times after that, sometimes to a kind master, sometimes to one who was not so kind. At last he fell into the clutches of the most feared and hated planter in the state of Louisiana—Simon Legree.

Simon Legree soon took a dislike to good old Tom. Before long this dislike turned into hate.

Then one day a woman fainted in the fields. Legree ordered her to get up, but she was too weak to obey. So he turned to Tom and held out his many-stranded whip.

"Whip her," he ordered. "Whip her until she obeys."

Tom refused. "I cannot," he said softly.

Legree couldn't believe it. Tom was disobeying a direct order. He swung the whip across Tom's face. "There!" he stormed. "Now will you tell me again that you can't do it?"

"Yes, master," said Tom, wiping away a trickle of blood.

This was too much for a man like Legree. Snarling like a maddened animal, he began to whip Tom.

"Do as he says," one of the slaves cried frantically. "Or he'll kill you by inches!"

"Well, then," Tom gasped, "I will *die!*"

By this time Golda was completely lost in the action. Each time that whip came slashing down across

Tom's back she winced. Her stomach lurched, and her hands, gripping the seat back in front of her, turned white.

Suddenly it was all too much. Not knowing what she was doing, Golda sprang to her feet. "No! No!" she screamed. *"Stop it!"*

All around people nudged each other. A few even chuckled at this over-intense little girl.

"Sit *down*," Regina begged, tugging at Golda's skirt. "You're making a spectacle of yourself!"

For a moment more Golda stood staring at the stage below. Then slowly she sank back into her seat. For the rest of the play she sat quietly. But she heard not a single word more. She was too filled with horror—with the sense of outrage she would always feel when she was forced to witness an act of senseless cruelty.

Golda could do nothing to help old Tom—he was just a make-believe character on a stage. But a few months later, Golda found something else that stirred her sense of outrage. Something, perhaps, that might be able to be changed.

Schools in Milwaukee were free. But schoolbooks were not. Some children in Golda's class could afford to buy new books. Some, like Golda and Regina, had to be content with second-hand ones. But some children couldn't afford even the most battered of books. So they had to stand up in class and say that they didn't have money enough to pay for their own. Then they were supplied out of a special school charity fund.

Some of the boys and girls didn't mind admitting this in public. But Golda could tell that others were terribly embarrassed. It just wasn't fair! Why should people be humiliated this way—just because they were poor?

But what could be done about it? Golda began to toy with an idea. "Wouldn't it be wonderful if we could somehow raise the money to buy some books?"

"Sure it would be wonderful," Regina answered lightly. "So would roast beef for dinner every night. But you know how poor people are around here."

Golda nodded. The people in her neighborhood were poor, yes. But then so were her parents—almost as poor as they'd been in Russia. Yet somehow *they* managed to put aside a little each week for people who were even poorer than they were.

If Mama and Papa could do this, others could, too. A few pennies here, a quarter or two there . . .

Golda rounded up the other girls in her class. Then she explained her plan. "It's simple. What we will do is go door to door and explain the problem. Then we'll ask for whatever they can give."

"But that's *begging!*" one girl sputtered.

"So?" Golda answered calmly. "What's wrong with begging—for such a good cause?"

A few of the girls continued to hesitate. But Golda soon had most of them talked into it.

"When do we begin?"

"What's wrong with right now?"

"But first," Regina interrupted, "we should have a name. Or people might not take us seriously."

So they tackled this problem immediately.

"I know," one girl exclaimed. "What about calling ourselves The Young Sisters Society?"

There was a chorus of approval.

"Yes," Golda murmured, tapping a pencil against her teeth. "That's good. But . . . I know! We're also Americans! So what about The *American* Young Sisters Society?"

The American Young Sisters started the next afternoon. They went from door to door in their neighborhood, explaining their mission and asking for donations. Most of the people they talked to found their story very touching. They were willing to give what they could. A few, of course, just couldn't be bothered. They were too busy, they said. Or too poor to give.

Most of the girls accepted these refusals meekly. But not Golda. She wasn't rude—she'd just stand there until the lady of the house was forced to look her straight in the eye. Then she'd say quietly, "I was not born among counts and royalty either." Few people found they could refuse after that!

Day after day the Young Sisters' collection of coins grew bigger. Finally the box they were storing them in was brimful. Golda called a meeting and the girls separated the coins into proper stacks. They were amazed that they'd collected so much. It was time to carry out the final phase of their project.

The girls bought a big pile of old textbooks—very old textbooks. The covers were battered, and many of the pages were wrinkled and splattered with strange stains. But what did that matter? They weren't buying cloth bindings or paper. They were buying words and ideas. And these were as good as new.

The girls stacked the books in a corner of the cloakroom. Now anyone who needed a book could just go and pick one out—no questions asked.

Golda should have been satisfied. She *was* satisfied. But something still worried her. What would happen when this pile of books ran out? There wasn't any money to replace them. No, all that would be left then would be a good memory—and an empty corner.

Unless . . . As the months passed, Golda began to toy with an idea. Going door to door was all very well, but it would only work a few times. She wanted a way to raise money regularly, at least once a year. "And to do that," she told the girls of the American Young Sisters Society, "we have to give people something in return."

"But what?" a girl asked.

Golda leaned forward eagerly. "Entertainment, that's what! We'll rent Packen Hall and put on a show!"

The girls looked at each other. Golda had lots of

good ideas. But surely she was going overboard *this* time.

"Packen Hall?!!"

"But—but that's a whole big *auditorium!*"

"And the *money,* Golda. Packen Hall costs money to rent. Lots of money. And we're broke!"

Golda waved this problem away. "I've already talked to the manager. He says we can pay later."

"Pay later with *what?*"

"Why, money from the tickets we sell."

"But Goldie, even if we rent a hall, even if we put on a show, who'd come? Who will want to see a bunch of fourth-graders like us?"

Golda waved aside this worry, too. "Plenty of people," she said briskly. "If they're approached right."

So once more the Young Sisters whirled into action. Posters were painted and tacked onto lamp posts. Girls went from door to door, this time giving out handbills describing the coming ball. For that's what they decided to call the evening's entertainment—The American Young Sisters Society Ball.

Golda even managed to place an advertisement in the town's leading newspaper. "I'll pay later for it," she said to the grouchy-looking man behind the advertising desk.

At that moment the man stopped looking grouchy and began to look downright mean. "Now look, little girl," he growled, "we have a policy on this paper never to . . ." But then he looked up. Golda was standing there, looking so serious and trusting . . .

"Oh, all right!" he snapped. "But you'll have to have the money in by the end of the month!"

"Thank you," said Golda politely.

Finally the evening arrived. And Golda had been right. All sorts of people came. Some because their children would be performing. Others because they had nothing else to do that night.

And then there were the ones who came out of curiosity. They didn't expect to be entertained at all. They expected to be amused—amused by a group of ten-year-olds who had the nerve to stage a whole evening's entertainment.

One after another the Young Sisters performed. One girl read a story. Another recited poetry. A group danced a spirited folk dance. Another sang a rousing selection of songs.

Golda took part in several of these activities. But her main contribution was still to come. After the entertainment was over she was to give a speech explaining the more serious purpose of the evening.

The hour was growing late. By the time Golda rose to speak, many in the audience had grown restive. They were whispering and shifting in their seats, peering openly at their watches.

So at first Golda had a hard time capturing their attention. But she continued to speak—simply and soberly. And then something began to happen in that big, echoing hall. Years later, when Golda had become a famous person, people would try to figure out just *why* she was such a successful speaker. It wasn't because she had some sort of complicated way with words. Her words were always simple. And it wasn't because she was such a scholar.

Perhaps it was Golda's great emotional commitment to whatever she believed in. Whatever it was, it soon became plain that she could make people listen. She could also make them care.

Golda closed her speech by saying, "We of the American Young Sisters Society thank you for coming. We hope you had a good time." The audience broke into loud applause. More important, they also opened their purses and wallets.

As she came off the stage her mother and father were waiting to hug her. How proud they were! The evening—and Golda's first public speech—had been such a big success.

7

The Big Fight

That was a happy evening. There were many others for Golda and her family. For the Mabovitches had put down strong roots in Milwaukee.

"Our family never limited itself to matters of personal interest," Golda said years later. "No matter how busy she was, Mama always found time to help other families. Papa worked with his union, and for organizations to help less fortunate people in other lands. And everyone, even little Tzipka, was deeply involved in outside activities—discussion groups, clubs, political meetings, charities."

Many evenings a week everyone would be gone, attending one meeting or another. But one evening was different. On Friday everyone was sure to be home.

"I remember those Friday nights," Golda later

wrote. "There was always music and singing at the table."

And plenty of good talk, too. For it was a rare evening when a visiting lecturer or a political figure, a poet or a teacher did not come to share the Mabovitches' Sabbath Eve meal.

Such conversations! Often they would laugh and talk and argue far into the small hours of the morning. And Golda, fascinated, would fight sleep for as long as she could. But finally she'd drift off with their voices still rising and falling in her ears.

She was never surprised to wake the next morning and find one of these guests asleep in the living room. "We had a sofa in our home," she said, "and the intellectuals who slept on it gave it a sort of fame and honor."

But it wasn't just intellectuals who found their way to the Mabovitches'. Their home was a gathering place for all sorts of people—immigrants just arrived from Russia and Eastern Europe, Shaina's friends, people Bluma had met in the store and at the synagogue, Moshe's fellow union members. Even Golda's and Zipka's classmates were welcome.

Once Moshe brought home fifteen unexpected guests for dinner. Bluma didn't even look surprised. She just sent Golda to the kitchen to water the soup.

So life in Milwaukee was good. Golda loved everything about it—except for Mama's store. Bluma opened the store every morning at 6. Then she traveled across town to buy a day's worth of fruits and vegetables at the wholesale market. It was Golda's job to wait on early customers until she returned.

"Now don't worry, Goldie," Bluma would promise her daughter. "I'll be back in plenty of time for you to get to school."

But often she wasn't. Then Golda would be late. Sometimes once a week, sometimes twice, Golda would arrive long after the last bell had rung. Then there was nothing for the teacher to do but mark Golda Mabovitch tardy once more.

This just couldn't go on! Again and again Golda tried to explain that to Mama. It was like talking to a friendly but extremely thick brick wall.

"So what's the fuss?" Bluma would ask. "A few minutes here. A few minutes there. Especially when your grades are so good."

"Oh, Mama!" Golda would cry out. "That's not the point! Don't you *see?*"

But Bluma didn't see. "Look, Goldie, I am growing a little—no, a lot—tired of all this talk about school. What does it matter? After all, with school or without, you're going to grow up and do what every other girl does—get married."

Golda had been controlling herself carefully. But now all her good intentions flew to the winds.

"Oh, Mama!" she exclaimed furiously. "Don't be so old-fashioned!"

"Old-fashioned?" Suddenly Bluma's voice was dangerously quiet. "I'll tell you what else I am. I'm your mother—and I'll thank you to remember that."

Golda took a deep breath. "I'm sorry, Mama. But don't you see? It's so important!"

"Running this store is important, too," Bluma snapped. Then, thinking to end the argument, she said in a more reasonable tone, "Besides, Goldie, what's the use of all this talk? I'm sorry you're unhappy. But what can I do? You know you're the only help I've got."

It was true. Shaina was living away from home. Zipka was still too young to be of much help. There was Papa, of course . . . At first Moshe had said he wouldn't work in the store. But when he saw how overworked his wife and daughter were he volunteered to help in his spare time. This turned out to be a decidedly mixed blessing.

Moshe was a warmhearted, friendly man, but he was a terrible salesman. And he had very little sympathy for most of the women who came into the store—women who often gathered there for good gossip as much as anything else.

"Can I help you, ladies?" Moshe would say again and again. But they would simply wave him off.

And when they did get around to buying something, what would it be? An eighth of a pound of butter, a half cup of sugar, or maybe three breakfast rolls. Then, more often than not, they would say, "Charge it, please, Mr. Mabovitch." No wonder they made Moshe fume.

But what really enraged him were the customers

he called "the feelers." These were the ladies who poked apples to see if they'd gone soft and pinched rolls to find out if they were still fresh.

Moshe would follow them around, scowling. But often they didn't take the hint. So finally he would say, "Look, if you have to pinch rolls there's a store right down the block. Go there and pinch. Here, I have to eat what's left over!"

Some of the customers did just that—and never came back. No, Papa wasn't the answer to Golda's problem. But there just had to *be* an answer. There just had to be! Things simply couldn't go on this way much longer!

Golda's teacher agreed. She began sending home notes to Bluma. Each one was shorter and sharper than the one before. Each one made the same point—Golda would simply have to arrive at school on time.

Bluma spoke English, but she had never learned to read it. So Golda read these notes aloud to her—one after another. Each time Bluma would listen with the greatest interest. And nothing changed.

Finally the teacher invited her to school for a chat. The teacher did most of the talking. Once more Bluma listened politely and nodded in all the right places. And Golda continued to be late.

Then it was report-card day. 'I'm sorry, Golda," the teacher said gently as she handed Golda hers. "I had no other choice."

That afternoon Golda arrived home in tears.

"What's the matter?" Bluma cried. "Are you sick? Do you hurt somewhere?"

Golda didn't answer. She just held out her report card. Bluma peered at it. Most of it meant nothing to her, of course. But she could make out some of the letters. "So many *A*'s! Your father will be very proud."

"Look at the bottom," Golda said in a strangled tone of voice.

Bluma did. "This is not an *A*," she said. "What is it?"

"It's an *F*."

"*F?* A failing grade? In what?"

"Punc-punctuality, Mama." Golda was so upset she stuttered.

"Punc-tuality?" Mama repeated the strange word. "What does it mean then?"

Golda couldn't help it. Suddenly something snapped. "It means *late*, Mama!" she shouted. "Late!"

Bluma's lips tightened—a sure sign she was getting mad. "Look, Goldie, I've had just about enough of all this. A report card tells no lies, true? And you have all *A*'s. In everything that matters, anyway. So I ask you again, what do a few minutes matter?"

Now Golda lost all control. "Oh! Don't you understand *anything?*" she yelled. "It matters! It's wrong! It's against the *rules!*"

Enough was enough! "Vestu vern a rebbetzin mit a tog shpeter!" Bluma yelled back in Yiddish. *So it will take you one more day to become a learned lady!*

Oh! Golda couldn't stand another moment of this! She whirled about and fled for her room. There she flopped face downward on the bed. Within minutes her pillow was soaked through with tears.

Again and again she tried to stop crying. But she couldn't. Tears were going to be a problem all her life. Whenever she was especially happy or sad or just plain frustrated, like now, out they would pour.

Finally the troubling situation was solved. Not by Golda or Bluma, but by a tall, grim-faced man who one day paid a visit to the store.

"Mrs. Mabovitch?" He fixed Bluma with cold, piercing eyes. When Mama nodded, he proceeded to lay down the law—literally. He was the truant officer for the city of Milwaukee, he announced. And it had been reported to him that Golda was often late for school. The laws of the state of Wisconsin, however, required that all children under the age of fourteen attend school regularly—and on time. So if Golda continued to be tardy, Bluma and her husband would be held responsible. Legally responsible.

It took a lot to scare Bluma. But that threat of the law did it. From then on Golda arrived at school on time.

So the struggle about Golda's education was over. Or was it?

8

Golda Mabovitch, Valedictorian

Golda was a natural student. From the very beginning she had been at the top of her class, and no one was surprised when it was announced that she would be valedictorian.

And so, one spring day in 1912, she sat on the stage of the school auditorium, dressed from head to foot in snowy white. The principal was speaking, welcoming the parents and other guests. But Golda knew that in just a moment he would turn and say, "Now I am proud to present our valedictorian, Golda Mabovitch."

The moment came. For a second Golda hesitated—struck by sudden stage fright. But then she rose and walked to the lectern. First she bowed her thanks to the principal. Then she turned to the waiting audience.

"Honored guests," she said. "We welcome you here today." Those first words came out a little stiffly. Then suddenly everything was all right. For Golda never found it very hard to speak in public. Before long she was deeply engrossed in her speech.

Moshe and Bluma were sitting in the audience, gazing up at their daughter. Every once in a while they would turn to each other and beam with pride.

Moshe Mabovitch was thinking how handsome his Golda looked, standing there so slim and straight in her long white gown, her heavy chestnut hair looped over her shoulder in a thick braid. And how mature. She was only fourteen. But already she looked much more mature than most of her classmates. Especially now, with her fair skin flushed with health and excitement, and her deep blue-gray eyes glowing with the seriousness of what she was saying.

Golda was talking about life—and what a person should expect from it. A life that was really worth living, she said, was one that was intellectually and socially useful. To prepare a person for such a life was education's highest purpose.

"Such pretty words," her mother thought. Bluma should have known better. Golda never said anything just to sound pretty.

Now Bluma's attention began to wander back to her own thoughts. She was proud of Golda, of course. She was also relieved. Thank goodness all this nonsense about education was finally finished. Now Golda could take some nice sensible job like other girls. A secretary perhaps. Or maybe a bookkeeper. Or she could stay home and help full-time in the store. Until she got married, that is . . .

Bluma was due for a shock. That evening, after a celebration dinner, Golda dropped her bombshell. "I want to go on to high school," she announced. "And after that college. I'm going to be a teacher."

High school? College? Bluma couldn't believe her ears. Her reaction was immediate.

"Stop!" she exploded. "I've had enough of this talk about school, school, school! Golda, I've been very patient. But now I say no more! You've graduated from the eighth grade, right? Well, it's time you stopped all this and got a job."

"Look, Mama, I don't think you were listening to my speech today. I don't want to be a typist or a bookkeeper. I want to do something *important,* something socially useful."

"So being a bookkeeper isn't useful?"

"Of course it is, but—"

Bluma had had enough of this conversation. "No more buts! I tell you this conversation is at an end! So is any more talk about high school!"

Golda appealed to her father. "Please, Papa . . . It means so much to me. Try to make Mama understand."

But she had little hope that he would. One of the reasons Moshe and Bluma had such a happy marriage was that long ago they had worked out a system. Moshe made all the major decisions for the family. But Bluma made the decisions at home.

"Well, Goldie," Moshe began now, "you know that men don't like smart girls."

Golda's heart sank. She'd been right. Papa wouldn't help.

But now Moshe turned to Bluma. "Still . . . ," he said slowly, "if Golda wants this thing so much, I think she ought to go."

"Oh, Papa!" Golda flew into his arms and hugged him.

"Moshe, I don't—"

Moshe spoke more firmly. "Her heart is set on it, Bluma."

Bluma opened her mouth to speak. Then she threw her hands in the air. "All right! All right! How can I fight both of you? So go on with this foolishness. Go to school. I just hope you don't grow a set of rabbi's whiskers before you're twenty-one!"

The next few months passed quietly. Golda spent the summer working as a salesgirl in a department store. Then, in September, she entered high school.

Bluma said not one word in opposition. This didn't mean she was reconciled to the idea, though. Not at all. It was not in her nature to give up. As a matter of fact, during all those months of seeming calm Bluma had been busy scheming—hatching another plan "for Goldie's own good."

Golda and her mother were alike in many ways. But they had very different dreams. Golda wanted to be socially useful. Bluma wanted her to be safe and secure. Golda wanted to become a teacher. Bluma was sure that this was a dead end. It was something girls did when they were too plain to catch a husband.

Golda was only fourteen; but already she looked like a young woman. Not only that, she was popular and outgoing. Surely it would be easy for her to make a good marriage. As a matter of fact Bluma already had the man in mind.

His name was Mr. Goodstein. A few months before he had come into the store to pick up a few groceries. Golda happened to be behind the counter. They talked for a minute or two. Then he left.

But the next day he was back. And the next. Always he would linger to talk to Golda. Soon it became perfectly clear—at least to Bluma—that he was very taken with Golda.

So she wasn't surprised when he sought her out. In a very shy voice he admitted that he'd fallen in love with Golda. Now he was asking Bluma's permission to make Golda his wife.

At first Bluma hesitated. After all, he was a little older than her daughter. Well, to be honest, he was quite a lot older. But what was so wrong with that? Bluma asked herself. Often such a difference in age helped make a marriage better instead of worse.

Besides, there were other things to consider. Mr.

Goodstein loved Golda. That was important. And most important, he had a good business. He was in real estate, and each year he earned more than the year before.

"Of course Golda is very young," Bluma said. "Only fourteen."

Mr. Goodstein was also a very understanding man. He explained that he was willing to wait for a few years—as long as he and Golda had some kind of understanding, as long as she didn't go out with other boys.

Bluma agreed that this was sensible. So everything was settled—between the two of them at least. But Bluma realized she had one more thing to do. Break the news to Golda. This proved very difficult indeed.

She tried hints. Nothing happened. She tried stronger hints. Still nothing. So finally there was nothing to do but come right out and tell Golda everything.

"You *what?*" Golda yelled, when she understood what her mother was talking about.

"Now Goldie, there's no sense in getting upset. I told him he'd have to wait a few years, and—"

"Wait?" Golda was so upset she could hardly talk. "Wait for what? I don't even *know* him!"

"Well," Bluma said comfortably. "That can be arranged."

"Oh, no, it can't! This is the craziest thing I ever heard of!"

"Goldie, why are you being so stubborn?"

"Stubborn? *Stubborn?*" Golda was almost speechless with rage. "Mama, you simply have no right—no right to *arrange* a marriage for me!"

"Why not?" Bluma asked, honestly puzzled. "Marriages have been arranged like this for centuries. It's always been done this way."

"Always been done! Times are different now! This is 1912. Not the dark ages!"

"So, young lady." Suddenly Bluma's voice turned grim. "I'll tell you one thing that isn't different. If you marry a poor man you will very likely stay poor for the rest of your life."

"Oh, Mama," Golda cried in real despair. "I'm not afraid of being poor! What I *am* afraid of is wasting my life. It's my only life. I want to *do* something with it."

Suddenly the fight seemed to go out of Bluma, and she sank into a chair. "All right," she said quietly. "I'll talk to Mr. Goodstein. But Golda, remember this. You are young. Someday you will understand—when you have children of your own."

A few peaceful weeks passed. And then another storm broke.

As soon as Golda sat down to dinner that night she knew something was wrong. Usually her mother was full of cheerful chatter about the day's happenings. But now she just sat, tense and tight-lipped, not even eating.

Finally Bluma turned to her daughter and asked in

a deceptively mild voice, "Is it true that in Wisconsin lady teachers can't be married?"

Oh, dear! Golda had been afraid that Mama was going to find out about this. "Well," she began unhappily, "that's the rule *now*. But lots of people feel it's very unjust—and they're working to change it. I'm sure it will be different soon . . ."

Golda's voice trailed off. For Bluma was just sitting there, staring.

From then on nothing Golda said made any difference at all. Bluma simply refused to listen. Once more Golda appealed to her father. But he was as deeply shocked as his wife.

"What a thing to train for," he said. "To be an old maid!"

From then on her mother and father were at her constantly. She must be reasonable. She must give up this foolishness at once. The only peaceful hours she had now were the ones she spent at school. When she was home it was one tense scene after another.

Her father kept ordering her to stop school. Her mother cried. And when she wasn't crying, she was nagging. Golda spent more and more of her time in her room. But even there she wasn't safe. Whenever she opened a book to study, Bluma somehow seemed to know. She'd materialize in the doorway and say mournfully, "You'll ruin your eyesight with so much reading. But then, what does it matter? Old maids always wear glasses."

Golda grew more and more unhappy. Oh, if only she had someone to talk to! Finally she did what she'd done so often in the past. She turned to her sister Shaina.

Shaina was living in Denver, Colorado, now. And someone else was there too—Shamai Korngold, the boy she'd been so fond of in Russia. Shamai had come to the United States a few years ago. He and Shaina had met again and their friendship had soon deepened into love. Now they were married and the parents of a little girl.

So Golda poured out her woes in a long letter to Shaina. How Mama had picked a man for her to marry . . . How she was trying to sabotage Golda's dream of becoming a teacher . . . Everything.

"I don't know what I'm going to do," she ended. "Mama, especially, is driving me crazy. She hardly gives me a moment's peace."

Golda chewed on the end of her pen for a moment. Then she added a P.S. "When you answer, please send it to Regina Hamburger's house. It would only make things worse if Mama and Papa knew I was writing to you about this."

A few days later Regina handed her Shaina's reply. The letter was full of advice and encouragement. Of course Golda was too bright to stop school. Certainly she should train to be a teacher—if that's what she wanted to do with her life. And as for being married! Plainly she was too young for such foolishness.

Golda read and reread that letter, and the others that soon followed. They helped a great deal. But no matter how much they helped they were still only words on paper. They had no real power to change the multiplying problems at home.

Then one blustery November day in 1912, Regina slipped Golda still another letter from Denver. Golda could see at a glance that it wasn't from Shaina. It was from her husband, Shamai.

Golda's eyes began to sparkle as she read that letter. For this was more than encouragement. This was a way out!

"I say you shouldn't stop school," Shamai wrote. "You are too young to work. No, Golda, you have a good chance to become something. My advice is that you should get ready to come to us. We are not rich either, but you will have good chances here to study."

Oh! Such a plan had never even entered her head. But she knew in that moment that she would do it. She would run away!

But first she'd have to plan very carefully. If Mama and Papa found out anything about this, they'd stop her immediately. So everything would have to be done in the deepest secrecy. Except for Regina. Golda never kept secrets from this best friend.

Before she could go, there were problems to solve. The biggest one was money. Where would she find enough to pay for her train ticket west?

She had a little saved. But it wasn't nearly

enough. Regina lent her some more. Then a friendly neighbor added to the fund—no questions asked. But still she didn't have enough.

"Well, there are always my immigrants," Golda said to herself. "I guess I can squeeze in a few more." For years now Golda had been teaching English to new arrivals in Milwaukee—at ten cents a lesson.

So slowly, in dimes and quarters and crumpled dollar bills, Golda gathered together enough to buy a one-way ticket to Denver.

Now there was nothing to stop her, except for the knowledge of how much she was going to hurt her parents. "The main thing is never to be excited, Goldie," Shaina had written in her last letter. "Be always calm and act coolly." This was good advice—but as the day of leave-taking drew closer this good advice became harder and harder to follow.

Finally it was her last night at home. Right after dinner Golda went to her room and pulled an old valise from under the bed. Quickly she filled it with clothes. And then a few of her favorite books. Finally when the old bag would not hold another thing, she snapped the clasps shut.

Earlier that day Golda had hidden a coil of rope under her bed. Now she pulled it out and tied one end firmly around the bulging valise. There! That ought to hold. Then she raised the window and leaned out.

"Regina?" she whispered.

"Yes." A whisper came drifting up from the middle of one of the darkest shadows. "Hurry up—I'm freezing!"

Golda strained to lift the bag to the windowsill. Then slowly, slowly, she began to let it down the side of the house. Inch by inch the rope slipped through her clenched hands.

"Careful!" Regina whispered. "You're hitting the side of the house!" And finally, "I've got it!"

"I'll be down in a moment," Golda whispered as she slid the window shut.

But there was no way Golda could slip out of the house unnoticed. "Where are you going?" Bluma called from the kitchen as Golda was putting on her coat.

"Oh, just for a walk with Regina," Golda answered in what she hoped was a casual tone of voice.

"Well, don't be long," her mother said. "It's cold out there—and something tells me it's going to start snowing."

"I won't, Mama. I'll be right back."

Sharing the weight of the heavy valise between them, Golda and Regina walked the fourteen blocks to the railroad station. There they left the bag in the checkroom. After a tearful farewell with Regina, Golda returned home.

She wasn't surprised to find her mother and father still in the kitchen. Often they spent the entire evening there. Mama was bustling about, baking a batch of cookies for the B'nai B'Rith meeting tomorrow night.

Papa, comfortable in shirt sleeves, was sitting at the table reading a Yiddish newspaper.

Oh, it was such a cozy scene! Papa and Mama might be terribly old-fashioned. They might be impossible to live with sometimes. But that didn't mean she didn't love them, and dread hurting them with all of her heart!

Golda felt the tears starting. Sternly she ordered them back. Now was not the time to cry. Not when so much depended on how normal she looked.

But sharp-eyed Bluma must have noticed something. "What is it, Goldie?" she asked. "You look strange. Are you coming down with a cold?"

"No, no, Mama," Golda said hastily. "I'm feeling just fine." Quickly she pulled out a chair and sat down at the kitchen table. Her books and a loose-leaf notebook were there. Golda pulled the notebook toward her and began to write.

She looked as if she were doing her homework. But she wasn't. She was trying to write a letter, trying one last time to explain to her mother and father why she had to do this.

But how could she? If she couldn't explain in person—and God knows she'd tried—how could she expect a few words on paper to explain in her place? Golda stifled a sigh. The answer was simple. She couldn't.

But she had to write something. She couldn't just go away with no word at all. Finally, after several false starts, she wrote: "I must go to live with Shaina so I can study. Love, Goldie."

She looked at those words and she shook her head. How cold and bare they looked on the page. They were not nearly enough. But they would have to do. Tomorrow she would mail this letter, such as it was, on the way to the railroad station. Mama would get it about noon. But by then it would be too late. Golda would already be on her way.

But she wasn't. For there was one thing Golda couldn't control. The train itself. The Denver Express was due to arrive in Milwaukee at 11 A.M. But it didn't. Other trains came and went; other passengers streamed into the station and out again. But Golda just sat on a bench in the waiting room—growing more nervous by the minute.

The noon whistle blew. "Oh, dear!" Golda thought. "Mama will have the letter by now."

Again and again Golda checked the big round railroad clock on the wall. One o'clock came. And then two. Finally it was almost three in the afternoon! Golda couldn't stand the suspense for a moment longer. Trying to act as grown up as she could, she rose to ask the stationmaster if he knew anything about the Denver Express.

"Oh, *that* train!" he grinned. "It's almost never on time. But don't worry, it always comes—usually the same day it's supposed to!"

Back in her seat Golda began to think of all the terrible things that could happen.

What if the stationmaster got suspicious?

What if he called the police to report her as a possible runaway?

What if something dreadful had happened to the train?

What if it had been *cancelled?*

And finally the worst thought of all. What if Mama came racing through those doors to drag her off home?

Golda was so busy listening to her fears she almost missed the train.

"Hey, Miss!" the stationmaster called. "That's her now!"

At last! Hastily Golda lugged her bag across the station and out onto the platform. And there it was, the Denver Express, just chugging to a stop before her.

In a moment she was inside. With a sigh of pure relief she sank onto the prickly horsehair seat.

"All aboard!" the conductor called.

A whistle blew shrilly. The engine gave a mighty tug—and the train began to move.

9

"He Has a Beautiful Soul"

Clickety - clack - clickety - clack - clickety - clack –– the wheels of the train sang as they turned faster and faster. And with each turn Golda grew more excited. She felt like singing, or laughing, or shouting! She was really doing it! She was really on her way!

But as the train continued westward, Golda's excitement began to fade—to be replaced by more sober thoughts.

For what lay ahead? The past few weeks she'd been so busy scheming and planning that she hadn't had time to think about the future, about what life would really be like in Denver.

She and Shaina had always been very close. But almost four years had passed since she'd seen her sister. Many things could happen in four years. Perhaps

Shaina had changed. Perhaps because of her marriage the old closeness wouldn't be there. Perhaps . . .

When Golda stepped off the train she saw Shaina and Shamai waiting for her on the platform. Shaina rushed up and hugged her. "Goldie! Goldie! It's so good to see you!" Suddenly Golda knew that her fears had been groundless. The old closeness was still there.

The only flaw in Golda's happiness now was the thought of her parents. Before long she got a letter from Zipka. A letter that described exactly how Mama and Papa were feeling. At first Mama had cried a lot. And Papa had wandered around strangely silent. Then one day he said he did not want Golda's name mentioned in his house. Not ever again.

Oh, that hurt! But Golda was sure her parents would forgive her—in time. Meanwhile she was determined to be happy in Denver. Before long she was as busy as she'd ever been at home. The first thing she did was to enroll in the local high school. Soon she was occupying her usual position at the top of the class.

After school she was busy, too. In Milwaukee she'd helped Mama in the store. Here she helped Shamai in his business, a small dry-cleaning shop.

At seven the shop closed and Shamai and Golda walked home to supper in the tiny Korngold apartment. When the supper dishes had been washed, Golda would spread her books on the kitchen table and begin to study.

So the days and nights were busy in Denver. But they found time for fun, too. Several evenings a week, and always on Saturday afternoon, the Korngolds held a kind of informal open house for their friends.

All sorts of people were apt to drop by. Shaina and Shamai were so poor they found it a struggle just to make ends meet, but there were two things they never ran short of—hot tea and good talk.

There was always much laughing and joking and singing. But Golda liked the serious conversations best. Usually they'd start out quietly enough. But before long the little room would begin to rock with loud and sometimes angry voices. For everyone seemed to have such firm—and often decidedly different— opinions. Especially about politics.

Some of the young people were socialists. Others were followers of the economic principles of Karl Marx. A few were even anarchists—they believed the answer to mankind's problems was no government at all!

Capitalism, trade unionism, Marxism, socialism, anarchism, Zionism—so many "isms." Such a heady brew of political and economic theories! Golda listened to them all, thought about them, and began to make up her mind about what she believed in—and what she did not.

But Golda didn't spend all her time thinking about such serious things. Something else was happening in her life. Golda had always made friends easily. She was popular with people of all ages. But now she was making a new kind of friend—boyfriends! And she was loving every minute of it.

Later Regina Hamburger would write, "Four out of five boys that met Golda fell in love with her." That certainly seemed to be happening now. More and more of the young men who came to the Korngolds for "tea and talk" considered Golda Mabovitch the nicest thing to hit Denver in years.

One after another they hastened to tell her so. Soon Golda had more invitations for dates than she could accept. She was out almost every night of the week with a different young man, sometimes until very late. There was no doubt about it, Golda was having the time of her life.

Golda might be. But Shaina was not. She was appalled by Golda's late hours, and the number of young men she was dating. Shaina was twenty-five years old now. And Golda was not yet sixteen. Hardly more than a child, Shaina thought. There was no doubt about it, she felt it was her plain duty to take care of Golda—whether Golda wanted to be taken care of or not.

Golda did not. She felt perfectly grown up. More important, she felt free for the first time in her life. And she was determined to protect this new-found independence at all costs.

At first Shaina just made comments—which Golda tried to ignore. But they were both very stubborn, and both very sure they were right. Before long they were fighting more and more.

Finally one night Golda and Shaina had the fight

of all fights, the one that could not be ignored or laughed away later on.

It was early evening, and once more Golda was preparing to go out.

"You've been out five nights in a row!" Shaina exploded. "You can't go out again!"

"Why not?" Golda asked.

"It's not good for you! Think of your health!"

"My health's fine."

"Then think of your reputation. People will talk!"

"So let them." Golda knew she wasn't doing anything wrong.

"Goldie, you've simply got to listen. Staying out so late—it's just not done!"

"Do you want to know what I think?" Golda snapped. "I think you've forgotten what it's like to be young!"

If Golda had worked on it for hours, she couldn't have picked a better way to outrage Shaina.

"This is my home," Shaina shouted, "and I order you to stop all this foolishness. Right now!"

"You know what you sound like?" Golda shouted right back. "You sound just like Mama. And I didn't come all the way to Denver to get that!"

There was a sudden moment of shocked silence. Then "So leave!" cried Shaina.

Shamai stepped forward quickly. He held out his hands. "Shaina, Golda," he begged. "You're both upset. You're both saying things you don't mean. So wait till tomorrow. Wait till you're calmer to talk any more.''

Neither sister seemed to hear him. They were much too angry to listen to good advice. And yet there was still one last moment when everything could have been made right. If either of them had said a kind word . . . or even held out her hand . . . But each waited for the other to make the first move. Each waited too long.

A moment later Golda banged out the front door—so furious that she took nothing with her, just the clothes on her back. For the rest of the week she stayed with friends. But soon she got a job as a clerk in a department store, and with her first paycheck she rented the smallest, cheapest room she could find.

Things were certainly not working out according to plan. Golda had come to Denver so she could go to high school. Now she had to quit school because of her job. Again and again she'd told her parents she wanted to be socially useful. Now she was working as a sales-girl in a store. And instead of the Korngolds' cheerful apartment, she was living in one small dingy room.

Plainly this should have been a perfect prescription for misery, but Golda wasn't miserable at all. As a matter of fact she was blissfully happy. There was a reason, of course. His name was Morris Myerson.

Golda had been happily playing the field for months. Now she began to turn down one date after another. Soon she was only going out with Morris. What was his secret, this young man who had captivated Golda so?

That was the question many of Golda's friends were asking. Golda was outgoing, gay, energetic. Morris seemed to be just the opposite. He was so shy and retiring that often, when the young people gathered for an evening of talk, he never said a word. But Golda noticed that when he did speak, the others always listened. For what he had to say was intelligent and to the point.

Golda couldn't have loved him for his money. He was as poor as everyone else. And even she had to admit that he wasn't exactly handsome. He was thin and stoop-shouldered. Thick glasses distorted his kind brown eyes. He was only twenty, but already his hair was beginning to thin at the top.

But Golda saw something deeper than looks or a surface social personality. "He has a beautiful soul," she wrote her friend Regina.

"I think you're falling in love," Regina wrote back.

Golda smiled to herself. She wasn't falling in love. She already had!

Most of the young men Golda had dated were primarily interested in things like politics and economics and social causes. Morris was much more interested in the arts. Often he would take Golda to free concerts in the park and to lectures on literature and art.

They also spent many evenings in the public library, reading and discussing books. He might be quiet with a group. But it was Morris who did most of the talking when they were alone. He felt that Golda's cultural education had been woefully neglected, and he was determined to remedy this situation.

Morris made out a list of good books for her to read. "And that's just a start!" he said as he handed it to her. Golda sighed when she saw the length of that list. But she took it meekly, and tried to read every book.

Golda didn't hesitate for a moment when Morris asked her to marry him. They both realized, however, that the wedding couldn't take place right away. Golda was just sixteen, and they both felt it would be better to wait a year or two.

Then one day a letter arrived from Milwaukee. As soon as Golda picked it up her eyes widened with astonishment. It was from Papa! He—who would not even let her name be mentioned in his presence—was writing a letter to her!

Quickly Golda tore open the envelope. And she was even more surprised by what was inside. Somehow Moshe and Bluma had heard that Golda was no longer living with her sister. They also knew that she'd been forced to quit school, take a job, and live by herself in a tiny room. This news had upset them greatly—enough to make them forget old grievances and do a complete about-face.

They wanted her to come home. Now. She could

continue her education. She could even train to be a teacher—if that's what she still wanted to be. They just hoped she would want to come home.

Of course she wanted to! Until this moment Golda had not allowed herself to feel how much she had missed this family of hers. Now those feelings came alive with a rush. And she had never really forgotten her dream of becoming a teacher, either.

The only sad thing was leaving Morris. He would have to remain in Denver for a while. His sister was in a tuberculosis hospital, and he was her sole support. But he would follow Golda to Milwaukee as soon as he could.

It was a very different person who climbed onto the train this time. When she'd arrived in Denver two years ago she'd been little more than a child. Now it was a poised young lady who handed her ticket to the conductor and settled comfortably into her seat for the trip back home.

10

"The Most Successful Speech
of My Life"

It was good to be home. Golda quickly settled into familiar routines again—attending high school, helping her mother in the store, seeing old friends. And of course there was a new routine now—writing letters to Morris, and reading his in return.

In a personal way Golda had never been happier. But in those months after returning to Milwaukee she was reminded again and again that life is more than one person's happiness. For the year was 1914, and in Europe World War I had begun.

As always in wartime, innocent people suffered brutally—often more than the soldiers fighting in the area. But in this war too many of the people were Jews.

In the countries of Eastern Europe and in the part

of Russia where the Mabovitches had lived, German and Russian armies clashed again and again. To the Jewish civilians, it hardly mattered which side won a battle. The Germans and the Russians were bitter enemies, but they did agree on one thing—their hatred of the Jews.

Once more Jews were blamed for whatever happened. If the Germans lost a battle they said it was because the Jews in the area had spied for the Russians. If the Russians happened to lose they said the same thing—in reverse.

Once more there were reports of pogroms and persecutions. In Poland, Russia, and Romania—wherever the armies advanced—entire Jewish towns were looted and burned. Before long hundreds of thousands of people were left homeless and hungry. They wandered the countries of Eastern Europe with only one aim in mind—to stay out of the way of war. But all too often the terrible tide would sweep over them again. Suddenly and savagely.

The rest of the world reacted to these acts of cruelty, of course. Important people in many countries made indignant speeches. The speeches were applauded by other important and concerned people, and promptly forgotten. Newspaper articles were written, and forgotten too. Committees were formed to write elaborate and carefully worded protests. These protests were sent to the governments of Russia and Germany. And ignored by both.

In a more practical vein organizations were set up to help relieve some of the worst of the suffering. Golda threw herself into this kind of work. She spent many hours a week collecting money and clothing to be sent overseas. And more and more often she spoke, urging others to do the same.

But Golda was growing uneasy. As the war and the suffering went on, she began to ask herself some increasingly disturbing questions. She and her family and her friends were working as hard as they could to help. They were spending every free moment they had. Yet was it enough? For what would happen after the last bit of food they sent was eaten, the last piece of clothing worn out? What would remain then—except the problem?

Still, what else could she do? So Golda stifled her doubts, and kept on working.

Then one afternoon she came home from school to find her mother and father sitting in the parlor. Just sitting. Golda began to worry, for this wasn't like them at all, to just sit and do nothing. Especially in the middle of the afternoon.

A moment later she *knew* something was wrong. For now she could see that her mother had been crying. "What is it?" Golda cried. "Is it Shaina? Has something happened to Zipka?"

Finally Moshe Mabovitch explained. "Do you remember Pinsk, Golda?"

Golda nodded. Of course she remembered Pinsk.

How could she forget that muddy little town where so many of her relatives still lived?

"Do you also remember the big Catholic Church? The one right across from Grandfather's tavern?"

Once more Golda nodded, more slowly this time. "I think so . . ."

Then slowly, falteringly, Moshe told her that they had just received word from Pinsk that forty Jewish men had been lined up against the church wall the week before—and shot.

"Why?" Golda's voice was trembling with shock.

"Since when do they need reasons?" Bluma whispered through her tears.

"But *why?*" Golda asked again.

"It is said," Moshe answered, "that these men were part of a group distributing money and clothing to the refugees."

That night Golda did not sleep at all. She tossed and turned until her bedcovers were a tangled mess. Finally she kicked them off and sat up in bed. She stared into the dark, filled with outrage.

Since when do they need reasons? Mama had said that afternoon. It was true. And the problem was rooted in history itself. For centuries the Jews had been forced to wander from country to country. Sometimes they had been treated well—more often not. But wherever they had settled they had always been a minority. It was this fact above all others that caused so much hatred and distrust.

Again and again Jews had suffered because they were different, because they refused to give up their religion, their traditions, their cherished ways of life. Most of all, because there were so few of them in any one country, and so many others.

Well, it was time they stopped suffering! More and more Golda's thoughts turned toward Zionism. Zionism was a political theory. But it was more than that. It was also a very specific plan. A plan to build a homeland for the Jews in Palestine.

Almost two thousand years before the Jews had been a nation there. Then they'd been conquered and driven out by the Romans. From then on groups of Jews settled in many different lands. But always they yearned to go back again—back to their original homeland, Palestine.

"L' shanah ha-baah bi Yerushalayim," they said in their prayers. *Next year in Jerusalem.* How well Golda understood this yearning to return to Jerusalem, to Palestine! But what most Jews meant was that someday a Messiah would come and lead them home again.

The Zionists too said, "Next year in Jerusalem." But for them the words were no longer a cry of longing. They were a fiery challenge instead. For the Zionists were not saying *someday*. They were saying *now!*

With each passing day Golda became more deeply involved with Zionist activities. She went to meetings. She sold copies of Zionist magazines like *The Young Maccabean* and *New Judea*. She spent many hours a week on street corners collecting money for the Jewish National Fund—the organization that was buying land in Palestine from Turkish and Arab landowners. And of course she spoke. The Zionists of Milwaukee discovered soon enough about Golda's way with words.

Golda's mother and father didn't know what to make of all this speechmaking. On the one hand, they were very proud. Proud that Golda was so determined to help others. Proud that she was such a success. On the other hand, she was still a young girl. And they both had very definite ideas about what was proper for a young girl to do—and what was not.

Golda's father in particular was getting upset. He didn't mind Golda speaking in a school auditorium or a synagogue meeting room or even in a big lecture hall. But a few days before someone had informed him that Golda was speaking in other places, too. Places that simply weren't safe or proper for a young girl. Like parks and street corners!

Dinner was barely over one night when Golda asked to be excused. She began to put on her coat.

"Where are you going?" Moshe asked, peering pointedly at his watch.

"To make a speech, Papa," Golda answered.

"Where?"

Golda began to stall for time. "Well, it's really a rally . . . And there'll be lots of us. You know some of them. Isaak will be there, and—"

"Where?" Moshe asked again.

"Well, it's on the corner of—"

"What? A Mabovitch daughter in the street?"

"It's not *in* the street, Papa. It's on the sidewalk. And there'll be plenty—"

"Street, sidewalk." Moshe waved her explanations aside. "What does it matter? You're not going."

"But Papa, my friends are waiting."

"Let them wait."

"I can't do that."

The two stubborn Mabovitches glared at each other.

"You won't go," Moshe said. His voice was very stern. "For I tell you this, Golda. If you do, I'll come and drag you down by your braid!"

"I'm sorry, Papa," Golda said just as firmly. "I have to go. I promised." Then she slipped out the door.

Golda's voice had been firm. But she had the sense to be very worried. Her father was a kindly man, but he was also very strict. And he did not usually issue idle threats.

As soon as she got to the rally she warned her friends what to expect. She was determined to go on, whatever happened. "Watch for him," she begged. "Try to head him off."

A few minutes later Golda climbed onto a wooden crate and looked over the crowd. For a moment she thought she was going to be lucky. But then she saw her father standing on the far edge. His arms were folded across his chest and he was scowling fiercely.

Oh, dear! But people were waiting, and there was nothing for her to do but start. For the first few minutes Golda was very aware of that angry figure on the edge of the crowd. Then she became lost in what she was saying.

As soon as the speech was over, however, she looked toward the spot where he'd been standing. He was gone!

When Golda got home later, she found her mother in the kitchen mending some socks.

"Where's Papa?" she asked.

"He went to bed." Mama bit a piece of thread in two with her teeth.

"Did . . . did he say something?"

"Yes." There was a twinkle in Bluma's eyes.

"Well, *what?*"

Finally Golda's mother smiled. "He said, 'Ich vais nit fun vanit nemt sich dos zu ihr.' " *I don't know where she gets it from.*

Moshe never mentioned that speech to Golda. But he never interfered with her again.

In the years to come Golda would make many more speeches. Instead of street corners she would speak in vast halls and in palaces. She would address heads of state and some of the most important people on earth. Because of what she said the policies of whole nations would sometimes be changed.

But always that simple speech on a street corner in Milwaukee would remain clear in her mind. Again and again she would say, ''That was the most successful speech of my life.''

11

The Palestine Bank Accounts

If only Morris were so easy to convince. But he wasn't. Golda wrote him in Denver, telling him of her decision to become a Zionist. His answer was decidedly lukewarm.

"I don't know whether to say I am glad or sorry that you have joined the Zionist party," Morris wrote, "and that you seem to be so enthusiastic a nationalist. I am altogether passive in the matter . . ."

Oh dear, Golda thought when she read that letter, for there was something she hadn't told Morris yet. What would he say when he learned that she had committed more than her time and her abilities to the cause? What would he say when he discovered she'd committed her *self* too?

The basic aim of Zionism was to rebuild a country

in Palestine. To do that, one thing would be needed above all others. People. Many of Golda's Zionist friends talked of settling in Palestine—some day. But few really intended to go. The more honest admitted it. "Let the poor downtrodden Jews of Europe have the honor of pioneering," they said. "Meanwhile we will help from here."

But that wasn't Golda's way. If she believed in something she had to act on that belief. It wasn't possible to go to Palestine now, for war was still raging in the area. But she intended to go just as soon as she had the chance.

The only question now was what Morris would say. Golda didn't have to wait long to find out, for a few weeks later he arrived in Milwaukee.

As a matter of fact Morris wasn't very worried at first. Golda was still young. This was probably just the passing fancy of a romantic girl, a part of growing up. All he had to do was be patient. Time would take care of the rest.

Morris was making a mistake. Time only increased Golda's dedication to Zionism—and to Palestine. Still, he remained reasonably full of hope—until a man named David Ben-Gurion came to town.

Ben-Gurion was a Polish Jew who had immigrated to Palestine as a young man. Now he was in the United States, traveling from city to city. When he came to Milwaukee Golda and some of her Zionist friends went to hear him speak.

Most of the audience was not impressed. Standing before them was a small, untidy man with bushy brown hair and equally bushy eyebrows. "Why, he hasn't even bothered to put on proper clothes," one woman whispered to her husband.

By her standards it was true. For David Ben-Gurion was dressed in plain cotton pants and an old work shirt with rolled-up sleeves. Who could have guessed that one day he would be the first Prime Minister of Israel?

Ben-Gurion began to speak. He talked about the first wave of pioneers who had gone to Palestine only a few years before. They were farmers and workers and shopkeepers and scholars. They'd had nothing in common except that almost all of them were very poor. So there was no question of taking a train or riding in a wagon. They had walked all the way.

They walked through rocky valleys, and over rugged mountains where in winter the snow drifted up to their waists. They walked across the burning deserts of Syria and Lebanon and Turkey. They walked until it seemed they could not take another step. Then, if they were lucky, they would be taken in by some small Jewish community in one of the strange lands they were passing through. There they would rest. But never for long. Soon the urge to move on would grow too strong.

Finally, after months—or even years—they would arrive. To find what? Almost nothing. Once, long,

long ago, Palestine had been called the land of milk and honey. It had been a place of rich farmlands and green forests. But through the centuries the land had changed. Now there was only mile after mile of desert. In other areas there was nothing but bogs and swamps. Everywhere the hillsides were so bare and rocky that not even the smallest trees could put down roots.

A few couldn't bear what they saw, and went back to their old homes. But most stayed. For here, thousands of years ago, they had begun as a nation. Here they were determined to become a nation again.

But how were they going to turn all this mud and sand and rock into fertile land? It seemed an impossible task.

Ben-Gurion had been speaking in a quiet tone. Now, as he came to the heart of his message, his voice rose and his sentences became clipped.

Those early pioneers had worked out a way, he told his audience. No one person or even a family could have managed alone. So they had banded together into groups to farm the land. Each of these was called a *kibbutz*—the Hebrew word for "group."

A kibbutz was a practical way to conquer a hostile environment. It was also an experiment—an experiment in a new way of living. For life on a kibbutz was very different from life on a normal farm. Or life anywhere else.

First of all everyone was an equal. There were no bosses and no servants. And there was no such thing as a good job or a bad job. All work was considered honorable.

On a kibbutz everything was shared. Nothing was privately owned. Not the books a person read, not the bed he slept in, not even the shirt on his back. And the land he worked so hard to develop would never belong to him either. It would remain forever the property of the Jewish people.

So what did the kibbutzniks get for all this backbreaking, often heartbreaking labor? asked Ben-Gurion. Nothing . . . except a sense of fulfillment. That was enough for them.

"The way for Jews to reclaim their ancient land," he said, "is not by argument or by listing historical precedents, but by *labor*. By creating something fruitful where previously there was nothing."

"So come to us," he said in closing. "Come as soon as you can." Then, with a curt bob of his head, he strode off the stage.

There was a smattering of polite applause. But most of the audience was decidedly unimpressed by David Ben-Gurion *and* his message. Did he really expect *them* to go over there and grub in the ground?

Golda could hear their comments as they walked up the aisle.

"Far too extreme!"

"And very simplistic, too!"

"You're absolutely right. Life's much more complicated than he seems to realize."

Eight-year-old Golda solemnly poses for her first photograph in America.

LOUISE G. BORN

Classical Course; Girls' Club; Lincoln; Pageant.

"Ready to make a day of night, Goddess excellently bright!"

Louise Born.

HARRY MARTENS

Science Course; President M. N. D.; Football, '12, '14, '15; Senior Play; Track, '12, '13; Basket Ball, '12, '13, '14; Cap't. Indoor Baseball, '15.

"Has a smile for everybody."

Harry Martens

GOLDIE MABOWEHZ

Elective Course, 3 yrs.; Lincoln Society; Science Club; Pageant.

*"Those about her
From her shall read the perfect ways of honor."*

WILLIAM L. KICKHAEFER

Science Course; Lincoln; Gridiron; Senior Vaudeville, '15; Pageant.

*"Frequently seen in public places,
Social dances, sports and races."*

PEARL GILBERT

Commercial Course, 3½ yrs.; Palladium; Girls' Club.

*"The learning ear is always found
close to the speaking tongue."*

After a stormy courtship Golda and Morris
Myerson are married on December 24, 1917.

Opposite. Eighteen-year-old Golda (center) continues
her studies at the Milwaukee Normal School, but she
is increasingly involved with the dream of building a
Jewish homeland in Palestine. ("Those about her
shall read the perfect ways of honor" reads the text
beside her picture.)

Golda, working in the fields of the kibbutz Merhavia soon after arriving in Palestine. She always remembered these days as "the happiest of my life."

Below: It is May 14, 1948. Golda signs the Declaration of Independence of the State of Israel. "It seemed to me," she later wrote, "that no Jew on earth had ever been more privileged than I was that Friday afternoon."

Golda, serving as the first Israeli Minister to Moscow, is mobbed by more than 50,000 fellow Jews outside Moscow's Great Synagogue on Rosh Hashanah, the Jewish New Year. "They would have hugged an Israeli broomstick," Golda commented later.

As the Six-Day War of 1967 draws to a close,
Golda visits the Western Wall. She is surrounded by
exhausted soldiers who have come to pray before all
that remains of the glory of Solomon's Temple.

But Golda was not interested in their opinions. Ben-Gurion's words had fired her with enthusiasm. "Come to us," he had said. *Bring us your brains. Bring us your bodies. Help us to build a new land. Work. Not talk!*

Golda realized her final problem had been solved. She'd known for quite a while that she must go to Palestine. Now she knew what she would do there. She would be a kibbutznik—a worker on the land.

If Morris hadn't been worried before, he certainly was now.

"A kibbutznik? A farmer? Golda, that's plain crazy! You're a *girl,* and not a very big one at that. Just what do you think you'll do on a kibbutz?"

"Anything they ask me to," Golda replied.

"Oh, Golda," Morris groaned. "Why Palestine?"

"Why *not* Palestine?" Golda answered. "It was our home. We came from there. Besides, who else wants it?"

That was true. Palestine had been many things to many peoples—a battlefield, a crossroads, a trade route, a winter grazing ground for goats and camels. But no one had ever loved the land itself, except for the Jews.

There were a few tribes roaming the desert. And some desperately poor Arab villages. That was all. Once Palestine might have been the land of milk and honey, but now it was a very barren spot on the map.

Morris took a deep breath. "Look, Goldie, this land you people are buying over there is terrible! It's useless!"

Which again seemed to be true. The rich Turks and Arabs who owned vast stretches of land in Palestine were not fools. They soon sensed how desperately the Jews wanted this land. So they sold only the very worst of it and charged huge sums even for that. Sums these poor settlers could never have paid without help from other Jews all over the world.

Golda nodded. "I agree. The land is terrible. But it is *not* useless, not if we work hard enough with it. Oh, Morris, don't you see? Already some of the swamps are being drained. Parts of the desert are being brought back to life . . ."

Morris raised an eyebrow.

"All right, all right," Golda said, "so it's just a beginning. But who knows where this beginning will lead?"

"I'll tell you where it will lead—to heartbreak! Even if you rescue a few thousand acres, a few hundred thousand, you won't have a nation. You'll *never* have a nation. The Turks may not be doing anything with Palestine. It may not be worth a thing to them. But they'll never let you set up a *government* there. All you'll have is some land in a forgotten corner of the Turkish Empire, not a country. This Zionist talk is nothing but a dream!"

Morris had many logical arguments on his side. But still Golda couldn't agree. For Zionism was *her* dream. And somehow she knew that it was better to work for a dream—a dream that might not come true—than to have no dream at all.

Again and again in the next few months Golda and Morris discussed this problem of their future. Sometimes they discussed it calmly, sometimes their voices rose in anger. But always the outcome was the same. With all his heart Morris wanted to stay in America, and with all her heart Golda knew she had to go to Palestine. They were as much in love as ever, but finally they realized their goals in life were just too different. They agreed that the only sensible thing would be to separate.

Golda had graduated from high school in the spring of 1916. In the fall of that year she entered Milwaukee Normal School for Teachers. But almost every day she asked herself, ''What am I doing here? What good will an American teacher's certificate be on a kibbutz in Palestine?''

The answer, of course, was none at all. So before the first year was over Golda dropped out of college. From then on she would devote all her time and energy to the cause.

Soon the Zionist organization Poale Zion offered her a job. The pay was only fifteen dollars a week. This was far less than Golda could make at many other jobs. Still, she accepted eagerly.

Golda spent most of her time helping to organize new Poale Zion chapters in Milwaukee and other nearby cities. After one of her trips to Chicago a friend wrote from there, "I hope you come back soon, for you are a good motor. You have the power of putting other people to work. Some people thrive on misery. You thrive on hard work."

It was just as well Golda was working so hard. For she missed Morris terribly. It was natural for her to be cheerful and outgoing. But often now she would fall into quiet, withdrawn moods. Whenever someone asked what was wrong, she'd answer, "Nothing." But her best friends understood. It was the break with Morris.

Then, in the autumn of 1917, two wonderful things happened to Golda. The first was personal. Morris had been just as miserable without Golda as she'd been without him, and now he came to a decision. He simply could not live a life without her. He would even go to Palestine, if that's what she still wanted.

Now nothing stood in the way of their happiness! "Let's not wait any longer," Morris urged. Golda agreed. Their wedding date was set for December 26, 1917.

The other thing that happened in the fall of that year wasn't personal at all. It was an international event that would eventually change the lives of millions of people. The English and the Turks were still fighting in the Middle East, but an English victory was clearly in sight. When that happened England would control a vast area—including Palestine.

Now, on November 2, 1917, the British Foreign Secretary, Arthur Balfour, announced: "His Majesty's Government view with favour the establishment in Palestine of a National Home for the Jewish people . . ."

What incredible news! A home for the Jewish people. Those eighteen words were like a miracle—a miracle that turned the Zionist dream into a political reality.

Not right away, however. First, the British Foreign Secretary said, Jews would have to live in the area for a number of years. They would have to build farms and industries, schools and hospitals, and all sorts of governmental institutions. They would have to prove that they could continue as a country on their own. Then the English would leave.

But what did a few years matter? After all, the Jews had waited almost two thousand years already. They could afford to wait a few more. The important thing was that it was going to happen. Not in some foggy future, but within their own lifetimes!

Now Golda's enthusiasm became boundless. It began to affect her friends. Several of them announced that they would like to go to Palestine too.

One of these friends was Regina Hamburger. Years later she said, "Why did I go to Palestine? Well, I went first for Zionism. Second, because I thought it might be fun. And third—why, because of Goldie, of course."

As each person announced his intention to go,

Golda would say, "Fine! You know what you have to do first." Save money, that was what. Several years ago Golda had opened a special savings account at the bank. She called it her Palestine Bank Account, and every week she put what she could in it. She knew she'd need a great deal of money for her passage to Palestine, and more for living expenses until she could settle on the land.

Now more Palestine Bank Accounts were opened, and everyone settled down to the hard work of filling them. Golda stayed at her job with Poale Zion. Regina worked as a secretary and also clerked in a shoe store at night. Yossel Kopelov, Regina's boyfriend, was a barber. Morris painted signs.

The weeks became months, and the months became years, while they scrimped and saved and worked. It took them almost four years. But at last they did it—at last there was enough saved up. Tickets were bought on the S.S. *Pocahontas,* sailing from New York City on May 23, 1921. The great adventure was about to begin!

But first there were some special good-byes to be said. Golda and her sister had long since made up that silly fight they'd had in Denver. Now the Korngolds lived in Chicago, and Golda and Morris journeyed there for one final farewell.

That was a happy evening. Golda was too excited to sit still. She danced back and forth across the room, all the while bubbling over with facts and stories about

Palestine. "Just think!" she kept saying. "Just think!"

Shaina was sitting quietly, sewing a tear in one of her son's shirts. As Golda talked her needle slowed . . . and finally stopped. Her face began to glow. Without even knowing she was saying it, Shaina began to echo Golda. "Just think . . . Just think . . ."

Shamai looked at his wife—and made what he later called his one big mistake. "Perhaps you would like to go too?" he asked.

He was joking, of course. After all, Shaina was no young girl to go traipsing off halfway around the world. She was past thirty now—a married woman with two growing children to take care of.

But Shaina didn't hesitate. "Yes," she answered steadily. "If you will give me the money."

Even Golda was shocked into silence! For what a decision that was! Golda knew that Shaina was as deeply in love with her husband as she'd been on their wedding day. Even being apart from him for a few days caused her deep pain. Yet now she was talking of a separation that might last for months, even years.

For Shaina might go to Palestine, and even take the children with her. But Shamai would not be able to go. He would have to stay behind in America and send money from there.

Suddenly Shaina jumped to her feet. The color was high in her cheeks, and her eyes were sparkling dangerously. "What's everybody so startled about?" she snapped. "Look Goldie, you've been talking about

Palestine for years! But that doesn't mean you own it! After all, who was the first revolutionary in the family, anyway?''

Then her expression softened as she turned toward her husband. "I have to go," she said quietly, her hand outstretched. "Please understand."

For several moments Shamai just stared at her. Then he too held out his hand.

The next morning Golda and Morris traveled to Milwaukee for a last visit with her parents and Zipka. Moshe and Bluma had not protested when Golda announced her decision to settle in Palestine; as a matter of fact, they planned to join her there in a few years. But that didn't make this moment of parting any easier. A few years was a long time.

So as they stood on the platform of the train station Bluma was crying, of course. So was Golda, a little. But as she turned toward her father she was suddenly deeply touched. For he was crying too, right there in public. "Oh, Papa," Golda murmured. She'd never seen him cry before. She never would again.

Finally the day arrived. They all stood by the ship's rail—Golda and Morris, Shaina, Regina, and all the others who'd been stirred by Golda's enthusiasm. All around, people were laughing and chattering and calling final good-byes to friends on the dock below. But Golda just stood there, quiet and somehow withdrawn.

For she too was busy saying good-bye. Good-bye

to fifteen years in America. They'd been busy years, happy years, and she would never forget them.

So many memories came to mind—Papa waiting on the platform when they arrived in Milwaukee . . . that first sight of the house on 6th and Walnut streets . . . her friend the Chinese next door . . . the first day of school . . . she and Regina sneaking off to see *Uncle Tom's Cabin* . . . the American Young Sisters Society . . . all those fights with Mama about school . . . running away to Denver . . . her first date with Morris . . . the speech on the street corner . . .

So many good memories, so few bad ones.

The ship had moved slowly down the Hudson River. Now it was passing the Statue of Liberty. Years ago in school Golda had learned the words that were carved into the base. They came to mind again.

"Give me your tired, your poor,
Your huddled masses yearning to breathe free,
The wretched refuse of your teeming shore.
Send these, the homeless,
    tempest-tossed to me . . ."

Golda gazed up at the torch in the statue's upraised hand, and said the final words aloud to herself. ". . . I lift my lamp beside the golden door."

She shivered with pure feeling. For that's what America had been to her. A golden place. She'd come as a scared little immigrant girl of eight. Now, fifteen years later, she was a confident young woman.

Suddenly Golda swung around, away from the

Statue of Liberty and the receding American shoreline. Her good-byes to America were finished. The American years were behind her. Now, gripping the ship's rail, she stared eagerly out across the empty sea.

To what?

12

The Promised Land

"Okay, Golda . . . Now we're here. So let's go home."

It was Yossel Kopelov, Regina's boyfriend, speaking. And almost everyone laughed. But the laughter had a decidedly hollow sound to it.

Two months had passed since Golda and the others had sailed from America. Those had been difficult months. Months of mishaps and delays. But they were finally here! Here in the Promised Land. They were standing on the railroad platform of the city of Tel Aviv—the first Jewish city to be built in 2,000 years. Now, as they looked around, their spirits—already battered—sank even lower.

And no wonder. For Tel-Aviv was just a little cluster of one- and two-story buildings made of something that looked like mud. And that wasn't all.

"Where *is* everything," someone murmured. For there were no trees, no flowers, no bushes, not even a road from the railroad station to the town.

The only thing there was plenty of was sand. As if to emphasize all this emptiness, in the distance there was a camel caravan winding its way out of sight around a sand dune.

For a moment Golda remembered something that had happened the night before. They had been on the train, crossing from Egypt into Palestine. At the border an immigration official came onto the train to inspect their papers. After stamping the papers he looked at them gloomily. "Oh, you people," he said, "when will you ever learn? What do you want to go to Palestine for? There's nothing there. No jobs. No places to stay—nothing. You, for example." He pointed to Golda. "What will you do?"

"I am going on the land," Golda answered proudly.

The man began to laugh. Then he turned away, muttering, "You'll see . . . You'll see . . ."

Golda gave herself a shake. What was she thinking of that dreary little man for? They were *here!* And suddenly she saw a man plodding toward them through the sand. "Welcome to Tel-Aviv!" he called out cheerily.

The pioneers' spirits lifted a little. He introduced himself as the owner of the only hotel in town. "And where do you come from?" he asked.

"America."

"Ah," the hotelkeeper said happily. "We do not get many of you people here. But come. Come. It's not wise to stand so long in the sun. Especially for newcomers!"

So Golda and the others picked up their suitcases and trudged off through the ankle-deep sand. The Hotel Barash was much like the other buildings in town—not very big and not very clean. Everything was covered with a film of sand. "No matter how tightly I close the windows it gets in anyway," the hotelkeeper explained.

Everyone went to bed early that night—and woke the next morning in a more cheerful frame of mind. Everyone except Morris. "Well, I can tell you one thing Palestine's got plenty of," he said, even before he got out of bed.

"What's that?" Golda asked sleepily.

"Bugs," he replied as he scratched himself.

The next few weeks *were* discouraging ones. The American pioneers had read many books about the problems of Palestine. They had attended lectures where everything had been spelled out in great detail. They knew that Palestine was a primitive land. But they hadn't expected it to be *this* primitive!

It was truly undeveloped. Everything was waiting to be done. Houses needed to be built, roads developed, farms cultivated, jobs made. In Milwaukee all this had sounded thrilling. Now, faced with the daily reality, some of the group found that the thrill of pioneering was fading fast.

No matter how discouraging it was, though, Golda, for one, never thought of leaving. "I loved America," she wrote years later. "But once I reached the Land of Israel I didn't experience a single moment of longing. It felt so natural for me to be there!"

For most of the pioneers the worst problem was the lack of work. They'd come to Palestine to help build a new land. Now most of them couldn't even find a job.

This was one problem Golda and Morris weren't worried about. As soon as they arrived in Palestine they'd applied for membership in the Kibbutz Merhavia. Now they were waiting for an answer.

Finally a letter from Merhavia arrived. Golda tore it open happily. She started to read it. And then suddenly she stopped—shocked. Merhavia had rejected them!

They didn't give any reason in the letter. But later Golda found out what the reason was. The Myersons were Americans. Most of the kibbutzniks—people who worked on the kibbutz—had come from the countries of Eastern Europe. Their memories were of poverty and pogroms. But Americans! Everyone knew that Americans lived a soft and easy life—even Jewish Americans. They'd never faced the harsh realities of hunger and danger and death. As soon as the going got tough Golda and Morris would probably flee back to the United States, ready to tell their friends all about their careers as pioneers in Palestine.

But Golda was determined. Somehow she would become a member of Merhavia. So she applied again. And again she and Morris were rejected. Now Golda was really upset. "It's just not fair!" she fumed. "At least they should give us a *chance!*" And she applied once more.

But this was the last time. Merhavia had a rule that a person could only apply for membership three times. If he was rejected, the case was closed. He could never apply again.

Oh, how the days dragged as Golda waited for that final answer! Finally it came. Her fingers were shaking as she tore open the envelope. Quickly she scanned the message.

"Morris! Shaina! Everyone! Come quickly," Golda cried. "We've been accepted!"

Suddenly everything was a blur of excited talk and congratulations. After a few minutes someone asked, "But why did they change their minds?"

Golda laughed. "They probably got sick and tired of me refusing to take *no* for an answer!"

Someone found a half filled bottle of wine and some glasses. Everyone took a sip. Everyone except Morris. He just stood there—glass in hand—staring straight ahead.

The Kibbutz Merhavia was in the Valley of Jezreel. When it had been founded in 1911 the place was nothing but tangled underbrush and stagnant swamps. But root by twisted root the first kibbutzniks had dug and hacked the underbrush away. Then they had begun to drain the swamps.

But every victory had been won at a staggering cost. The swamps were thick with mosquitoes—mosquitoes carrying the dreaded disease of malaria. Often a third of the kibbutzniks would be lying in bed, first shivering with chills and then burning with fever. By the time Golda and Morris arrived at Merhavia most of those original kibbutzniks were no longer there. Some were dead. Others had been made old long before their time.

But the fruits of their labor were there to be seen. The underbrush had been cleared. The swampy land had been drained. Fields and orchards stretched away in every direction.

So life on the land would be much easier for Golda and Morris than it had been for the first pioneers. But there were still problems. "You must take quinine tablets at every meal," they were told the very first day they arrived. Most of the swamps were gone, but malaria was still a big danger.

There were other dangers, too. Merhavia happened to lie between two Arab villages. Most of the Arabs in the area were friendly to the Jews—but not all. A few hated them so much that they were willing to kill. "So don't wear anything white if you're going out at night," a kibbutznik warned. "Even a kerchief.

White makes too good a target for a man with a gun.''

Early the next morning Golda and Morris received their first work assignments. Morris's job was to dig rocks out of a nearby hillside. Golda's was to pick almonds. "The quota is a basketful an hour," she was told when she arrived at the grove.

Golda worked as hard as she could—but soon she knew she'd never make the quota. Before long she was only determined to do one thing. Keep working.

Every muscle in her body screamed for her to quit. Oh, how she ached! Oh, how she longed to lie down and rest. But she knew that the others were watching her. She knew they were wondering how long "the American" would hold out before she made some excuse to stop working. "Well, I won't," Golda muttered. "I won't!"

And she didn't. It seemed the day would never end. But finally the signal was given to gather the baskets and take them to a central storage house.

Yet for Golda the day was not over. "When I returned to my room in the evening," she later told a friend, "I couldn't so much as move a finger, but I knew if I didn't show up at dinner the others would jeer: 'What did I tell you? That's an American girl for you!' Oh, I would gladly have skipped that supper! The chick-pea mush we ate wasn't worth the effort of lifting the fork to my mouth—but I went!"

But I went. Those words summed up Golda's determination in the next few weeks. She picked almonds for a while. Then she was assigned to other jobs. Golda did each as well as she could. And little by little her body began to toughen, until finally one wonderful day she could keep up with the rest of the kibbutzniks.

Most of Golda's jobs involved back-breaking labor. But the hardest job she had to do in those first months was simply baking bread. Golda's mother had been known for her light hand with all kinds of breads and pastries. It soon became plain that Golda had not inherited that talent.

"Baking bread," Golda confided mournfully to an old-timer one day, "is for me one of the profoundest mysteries of life." But profound mystery or not, it was her job, and Golda was determined to master it.

Finally, after many lumpy failures, she turned out a loaf of bread that was fit to eat. "And *that*," Golda remembered years later, "was one of the proudest days of my life!"

There were many proud days for Golda at Merhavia. She took naturally to kibbutz life. All day long she and the others worked at their various jobs. Then most evenings after supper they gathered in the dining hall for a *cumzitz*—a wonderful mingling of singing and dancing and good talk. Oh, how Golda loved these sessions! Often, eyes shining, cheeks flushed, she would still be sitting up talking long after most of the kibbutzniks had yawned themselves off to bed.

There was no doubt about it. Golda was a true kibbutznik. It seemed to be in her blood. And the others responded to this zest of hers. "She cheered us when we were in the dumps," one man remembered. "She raised our spirits."

But there was still some grumbling—mostly from the women—about Golda's "American ways." These women prided themselves on living absolutely unfeminine lives. They were determined to think and act and work like men.

Golda thought this was nonsense. She was perfectly willing to work like a man. But why *act* like one? So sometimes on the Sabbath she wore silk stockings to dinner. And if her dress was wrinkled she insisted on ironing it before a cumzitz. Often she filled jars with wildflowers and placed them on the dining room tables.

Golda was very well aware of the grumbling about her American ways. And one day—as she said—"I got my revenge."

The water system at Merhavia was very primitive. It was simply a big tank of rain water out behind the kitchen. And it didn't always work. Golda remembered, "In the summer we sometimes used to go into the shower all covered with dust at the end of a day's work, open the tap, and nothing would come out."

Then everyone knew what had happened. A certain bolt had slipped in the machinery at the top of the water tower. Someone would have to climb the long, shaky ladder and adjust it.

Someone was almost always a man. This was one

job that most of the women at Merhavia avoided. But one day Golda was working in the kitchen when the water suddenly went off. Before anyone could send for a male kibbutznik she dried her hands, picked up a wrench, and crossed the yard to the tower. Without pausing she began to climb the ladder. High above the ground she made the adjustment and started back down again. As she neared the bottom she saw a group of women gathered around the ladder. And on their faces were almost identical expressions of astonishment.

"What's the surprise?" Golda said innocently. "I mean, why should an *American* girl need a man to fix a little thing like that?" After that there was no more talk of Golda's American ways!

One day Golda wrote a lighthearted letter home, telling her parents of her various jobs and experiences. She also mentioned that everything seemed especially productive at Merhavia this year. Why, just that morning one of the kibbutz cows had given birth to a fine, sturdy calf.

A few weeks later Moshe Mabovitch wrote back, "I'm delighted with all the news. Now when are you going to be as productive as the cow?"

Golda's expression grew sober as she read those words. For her father had put his finger on a very sore spot indeed.

Golda was so happy at Merhavia. In a very real way she had found her heart's home. But for Morris it was a different story. He was growing more and more miserable.

Everything Golda loved, he hated. It was as simple as that. Golda was a dedicated Zionist. Morris wasn't interested in a national home for the Jews. Golda loved to be surrounded by people. Morris was always much happier alone.

And all this sharing! Sometimes Morris thought if he were asked to share one more thing he would go crazy. Wasn't there anything in this terrible place that could belong to him alone?

Worst of all, though, was the lack of privacy. Morris liked to read. And take long, rambling walks. And be alone with his wife sometimes! Even such simple pleasures as these were next to impossible.

Only one thing held Morris at Merhavia—his deep love for Golda. But there was one thing he absolutely refused to do. He would not have a child—not while he and Golda still lived on the kibbutz. Like everyone else on a kibbutz, children had to lead communal lives. They spent a few hours a day with their mothers and fathers. The rest of the time they lived in a separate children's house. They were taken care of by one kibbutznik after another.

"But not my child," Morris said firmly. "No child of mine is going to be raised by a string of substitute mothers!"

Again and again Golda and Morris discussed this problem. Finally, after many sad sessions, they arrived at a compromise. They would stay in Palestine—but not on the kibbutz. They would settle down to a more normal way of life.

So after two and a half years—"some of the very happiest years of my life," wrote Golda—the Myersons left Merhavia. They settled in the city of Jerusalem. And Golda tried to be the kind of wife Morris wanted. She tried with all her heart.

But she failed. The next four years, Golda said later, were the most wretched of her life. The Myersons were poor. But being poor was nothing new to Golda. It was this life of so little meaning that made her so miserable!

Again and again Golda thought about her days on the kibbutz. And her heart twisted every time. For there she had been living with a purpose and a goal.

Then, in November 1924, a son was born. They named him Menachem. Menachem was a beautiful baby with bright brown eyes and hair. Golda thought his smile must be the dearest thing in the world. "He's our little *sabra*," she murmured one evening to Morris. This was what Jews were beginning to call children who were born in Palestine. Sabra is a Hebrew word meaning fruit of the cactus. This fruit is very prickly on the outside, but inside it is sweetness itself.

Two years later another child, named Sarah, came to complete the family. And these two sabras of Golda's did bring sweetness into her troubled life. But even they could not make the misery go away.

Golda loved her husband. She adored her children. But being a wife and mother just wasn't enough for her. She had come to Palestine to help fulfill the

Zionist dream. She had come to help build a future homeland! And now she was doing nothing. Nothing! How much longer could she bear this emptiness and sense of isolation in her life?

Then one afternoon Golda was on her way home from the vegetable market when she heard someone calling to her. She turned and recognized an old friend from Merhavia days.

They laughed and chatted happily for a few minutes. The man explained that he now worked for the Histadrut—the central trade union for Jewish workers in Palestine.

"And what about you?" he asked. What could Golda say? She murmured something vague and tried to change the subject. But she didn't fool her old friend.

"My God, Goldie, do you mean you're *retired?*" he asked. "Do you mean to tell me that *this* . . . ," he pointed to the basket of vegetables she was carrying, ". . . is all you've been doing for the last four years?"

Golda could only nod and hope he'd say no more. But the man swept on—disapproval and disbelief fighting each other in his voice. "Goldie, you of all people know that we can't afford such luxuries. You have abilities! Brains! You can work! You can really accomplish something!"

His words were like knives, each cutting and leaving a tiny wound. Golda could only murmur, "I know—I know . . ." And at last, "I must be getting home now." Then she fled.

Golda tried to forget that painful meeting. But her friend didn't. A few days later there was a knock on her door. It was a stranger with a message—for her. Would she come to the Histadrut office? An official there wanted to talk to her about something.

Next morning Golda was ushered into the official's office. He came right to the point. Would Golda be interested in taking charge of the Moatzot Poalot, the Women's Labor Council of the Histadrut? He warned her that the work would be complex. The hours would be long. And the pay, unfortunately, was very low. Did she want the job?

Did she? "When do I start?" she asked.

Golda never remembered how she got home that afternoon. But all her life she would remember the feeling of pure happiness that filled her like light air.

Of course she realized there'd be problems. Especially with Morris. But somehow she'd make him understand this time. After all, this was only a job—not a total commitment like living on a kibbutz.

13

Highlights of History

But it wasn't just a job. It was a beginning—the beginning of public life for Golda. From now on she would move from one job to another. And each would be more important than the last. From now on Golda's personal story would get more and more involved with the story of the Jewish people—and with the history of her time.

Of course this growing involvement in public affairs didn't make Morris happy. And he wasn't the only member of the Myerson family to resent Golda's career. The children suffered too. Especially Menachem. More and more often Golda was asked to take trips away from home. Trips that sometimes lasted for weeks and even months.

Sarah remembered those days, and how her brother

reacted. "Often he quarreled with mother," she said. "And actually held onto her to stop her from leaving the house."

Sarah minded too, of course. But after she grew up she was able to say proudly, "For such a mother it was worth it."

Those separations weren't easy for Golda either. But she always went—because she felt it was her duty. While on a trip to England she wrote to her sister Shaina, begging for understanding. "I ask only one thing. That I be understood and believed. My social activities are not an accidental thing . . . I am hurt when Morris and others say that this is all superficial. That I am trying to be modern. You can understand how hard it is for me to leave. But in our present situation I could not refuse to do what was asked of me."

But in our present situation I could not refuse to do what was asked of me. Golda meant what she wrote—and she wasn't exaggerating. All sorts of wonderful things were happening in Palestine. Just ten years before, Golda and the other American pioneers had arrived in the tumbledown town of Tel-Aviv. Now Tel-Aviv was a bustling city of 100,000 people. Most of the country's swamps had been drained. Many patches of desert were beginning to bloom. Roads were being built where nothing but camel paths had ever been before. Schools were being built everywhere. Modern hospitals served Jews and Arabs alike. More and more newspapers and magazines and books were being printed in Hebrew—a language that had been considered dead for thousands of years.

But the 1930s were also a time of growing tension. During those years much of the attention of the world—and especially of the world's Jews—was focused on Germany. For in January 1933 a little man with glaring eyes and a shoebrush mustache had come to power there. His name was Adolf Hitler. Before long he and his Nazi party would plunge the world into war. For Hitler had a dream. A dream of conquering the world.

Adolf Hitler was also an anti-Semite—he had a wild and unreasoning hatred of anyone who happened to be Jewish. As soon as he came to power, one of the first things he did was to order all books written by Jews burned. For weeks great bonfires blazed all over Germany. Then it was forbidden to play music by Jewish composers. Soon Jewish children were forced to go to special ''Jew Schools.'' Many could not go to school at all.

Then the signs began to appear. They were everywhere—in office buildings and restaurants, stores and trains and public parks.

''No Jews Allowed.''

''We Do Not Sell To Jews.''

''Jews—And Dogs—Not Welcome Here.''

By the mid-1930s half the Jews of Germany had been fired from their jobs. Whole families began to starve. Jewish shops were looted. Jewish homes were turned over to any non-Jews who wanted them. Gangs roamed the streets looking for Jews to beat up. And more and more Jews were being thrown into jail.

Before long the prisons of Germany were filled to overflowing. And still more people were being arrested. So new prisons were built—prisons that in a few years' time would be called concentration camps.

Of course many of the Jews of Germany wanted to escape all this. But Hitler was preparing to invade many of the other countries of Europe. Countries where other millions of Jews would also be trapped. So where could they go?

In the summer of 1938, President Franklin Roosevelt of the United States called for an international conference to be held in Switzerland to study the growing problem.

For Golda this was especially joyous news! America—the land of her growing years—had not forgotten that countries should have consciences too!

By this time Golda was a very important and well-known person in Palestine. So no one was surprised when she was chosen by other Jewish leaders to represent Palestine at the conference. Of course she was not really a delegate—for Palestine was not really a country. But she would be there! This time Golda took special pains to explain to Menachem and Sarah why she had to go away again. "This is not just another conference," she said. "It might be the last chance for millions of Jews."

She went to the conference filled with hope—

believing that at last the countries of the world would do something real to help Hitler's victims.

And then day after day she listened as, one after another, those countries refused to help. They all had fine-sounding reasons. And they all hoped somebody else would save the Jews. But not *them*.

Golda did what she could. In the next few days she spoke to many delegates, telling them of the terrible hardships the Jews were suffering—and what might happen to them soon. She begged the delegates to save these people's lives.

But now Golda discovered something distressing. Most of the delegates offered their sympathy. But that was all they were able to give. Sympathy. Shamefacedly they explained that they had been issued firm instructions by their governments *before* they came to the conference. These instructions could not be changed. So the answer had to be *no*.

"My God!" Golda thought, "what is the *point* of all this then?"

The only country that was prepared to help at all was the United States. And it would only take 27,000 people a year—when millions were in danger.

The last afternoon of the conference Golda held a press conference. She was only forty years old. But her face was worn well beyond her years. The reporters listened to her. They took notes. And most of them could not hide the pity they felt for this sad-faced woman—and the millions of people she represented.

One man tried to express how he felt. Golda

thanked him for his concern. "But you know," she said slowly, "there is one ideal I have in my mind. One thing I want to see before I die. And that is that my people should not need expressions of sympathy any more."

Then it was too late. In September of 1939, the war began. The most terrible war in the history of the world. Hitler's armies rolled across the face of Europe, conquering country after country. And wherever the Nazis went, more and more Jews were trapped.

By 1942 many rumors were coming from Germany and the conquered lands. Rumors so terrible that most people refused to believe them. But the Jews of the world did. "There is no Zionism save the rescue of the Jews," Golda said during those dark days. But there is one place that no one can be rescued from—the grave.

All across Europe, Jews were being rounded up and herded into boxcars. The cars were locked. And then they traveled to their terrible destinations. Dachau, Belzen, Auschwitz, Buchenwald—these were names filled with terror. For they were concentration camps—camps that had become more than prisons. They were factories of death.

By thousands, by hundreds of thousands, finally by millions, the Jews of Europe were systematically murdered. And still the Germans were not done with them. The efficient Nazis took the jewelry from each body. The gold fillings were knocked from teeth—at Auschwitz alone seventeen *tons* of gold were collected this way. Women's hair was cut off, to be made into wigs or used to stuff mattresses. Human fat was used for making soap. After this the bodies were burned and the ashes sold as fertilizer.

Before they were stopped the Nazis killed six million Jews—one million of them children. That was one-third of all the Jews anywhere in the world!

But at last the war was over. On May 8, 1945, Germany surrendered. Now most of the world went wild with joy. In New York City and Paris, in London and Moscow, cheering crowds celebrated and danced in the streets.

In Palestine too there was a deep feeling of thankfulness. But no one celebrated in the streets of Jerusalem or Tel-Aviv. Too much had been lost. "On that day we couldn't go out into the streets," Golda said, "knowing as we did that a whole third of our people was no more."

But what about the ones who had somehow remained alive? What would happen to these survivors now? Most of them were displaced persons. Their homes were destroyed. Their businesses stolen. Their families dead. Now most of them turned with real longing toward Palestine. The Promised Land! That's where they wanted to try to begin life anew.

But there were two obstacles standing in the way of their coming. The British government. And the

Arabs. There had always been two groups of Arabs in Palestine—the very rich and the desperately poor. The rich were a tiny group who owned great stretches of land. The poor peasants had almost nothing—no education, no money, no rights. They lived more like slaves than free men.

In the early days, both these groups had been happy to see Jews come to Palestine. The rich Arab landowners had been eager to sell the worst land they had to "the crazy Jews"—and at incredibly high prices. The poor peasants had been happy too—for they soon realized they could learn many things from the newcomers. Jewish kibbutzniks taught them new ways of farming. Jewish doctors treated the sick. Jewish teachers taught some of the Arab children to read and write. But most of all the Jews set an example—an example of how to live a decent and dignified life.

And this scared the rich landlords. What if the Arab peasants began to want more out of life? What if they began to demand lives of decency and dignity too? There was only one way to stop all this from happening, the rich Arabs decided. They must keep any more Jews from coming to Palestine—and get rid of the ones who were already there.

The Arab landowners and politicians knew that their peasants were easily led. So they began to send agents into the cafes and coffee houses and religious meeting places. These men began to spread lies about the Jews. The peasants were very religious. So the agents said the Jews planned to attack their religion—burn down their holy places and destroy their faith. They also said the Jews were going to steal the peasants' land. This was an especially strange lie—since almost none of the peasants owned any land in the first place.

At first this hate campaign had little effect. The poor Arabs weren't eager to turn against their Jewish neighbors. But it doesn't take a great many people to start trouble. It takes a leader. And the wealthy Arabs had one. His name was the Grand Mufti. He knew just how to accomplish what they wanted. He told the peasants that from now on all Arabs in the world would share a sacred mission—a ''holy war'' against the Jews. And slowly more and more Arabs began to believe him—and to hate their old neighbors.

Meanwhile, all through the 1920s and 1930s the Arab landowners and politicians were putting pressure on the British government.

England's job in Palestine was to guide the Jews toward statehood. This was what had been promised with the Balfour Declaration of 1917. That document very clearly stated that ''His Majesty's government view with favour the establishment in Palestine of a national home for the Jewish people, and will use their best endeavors to facilitate the achievement of this object . . .''

But more and more the British were backing away from that promise. There were so many Arabs in the area after all. And so few Jews. Besides, the Arab countries had so much oil—oil that England wanted very much.

Before World War II the British government had bowed to Arab pressure and sharply limited the number of Jews who could come to Palestine. Because of this countless Jews had died under the Nazis who might have been saved.

But after all that had happened in the concentration camps, surely the British would change their minds now and let the ones that remained come to Palestine. Surely they would at last keep their promise of a homeland for the Jewish people in Palestine. Surely now they would stop playing politics with human lives!

But still England hesitated. Finally the British government offered to set up a joint Anglo-American Commission to study the problem. Whatever the commission decided, the British government promised to follow its advice.

Representatives of both the Arabs and the Jews would get a chance to present their case. And one of the most important speakers for the Jews was Golda Myerson.

She spoke to the commission about the goal of the early Jewish pioneers—the creation of a new society based on equality, justice, and cooperation. She told how they tried to achieve this goal in friendship with the Arab population. She told of their feeling of helplessness as millions of their fellow Jews were murdered by the Nazis—Jews who would have lived if they could have come to Palestine.

"I don't know, gentlemen, whether you who have the good fortune to belong to the two great democratic nations, the British and the American, can, with the best of will to understand our problems, realize what it means to be a member of a people whose very right to exist is constantly being questioned. . . . We Jews only want that which is given naturally to all the peoples of the world, to be masters of our own fate . . . to have the chance to bring the surviving Jewish children, of whom not so many are now left in the world, to this country so that they may grow up like our youngsters who were born here—free of fear."

Later, one of the commissioners asked her, "Mrs. Myerson, if the Jews could have the same privileges as a minority that you promise the Arabs as a minority would they be content?"

"No sir," Golda answered with great firmness. "Because there must be one place where Jews are *not* a minority. I believe that the Jews have come to this situation of helplessness and persecution and lack of dignity in their lives because of this curse of being a minority all over the world. There must be one place where their status is different."

Many more questions followed. Finally it seemed the session was over. But then Judge Hutcheson of the United States leaned forward. "One more question before you go, Mrs. Myerson . . ."

Golda sighed. She was so tired! But she nodded politely. "I've been wondering all afternoon," the judge asked, smiling. "Where did you get such a fluency in English?"

Golda grinned back. "Oh, that's easy to answer! I come from Milwaukee, Wisconsin!"

On May 1, 1946, the Anglo-American Commission issued its report. Every single member—British and Americans alike—said that 100,000 refugees should be admitted to Palestine immediately. And more than that, they said that the question of statehood for Jewish Palestine should also be seriously studied.

And then . . . the British went back on their promise. The Grand Mufti was stirring up trouble again. He and other Arab leaders announced loudly that if more Jews were allowed in the area they would cause as much trouble as they could. "It would take a full division of English troops to put down those Arab riots," Foreign Secretary Ernest Bevin explained to the world. So he rejected the commission's suggestions. England just could not allow such a situation to develop.

Jewish Palestine exploded! So the Foreign Secretary didn't want trouble. They'd show him what trouble was! He was worried about how many troops it would take to keep the peace in Palestine if more Jews were admitted. Well, they'd show him just how many troops it would take to keep them out!

David Ben-Gurion, the foremost leader of Jewish

Palestine, said, "We will act like a country until we *are* a country." He was calling for open rebellion!

And Golda agreed with him. "It is hard for us," she said to the British. "We don't want to fight you. We want to build, to construct. We want to enable the remnant of our people, those few who remain, to come here in peace. But if not—then you must understand in the clearest possible manner. We have no choice."

No choice. The words thrilled and electrified the Jews of Palestine. They scared plenty of people, too. For how could tiny Palestine fight a powerful country like England? And what about the Arabs? There were 50 million Arabs in the Middle East. And only 60,000 Jews. No, the odds were just too great. The Zionists must be reasonable. Or they would lose everything.

But the Jews of Palestine were tired of being reasonable. "I can honestly say that I was never affected by the question of the success of an undertaking," Golda said. "If I felt it was the right thing to do, I was for it regardless of the possible outcome." The Jews of Palestine refused to write "the end" to their dream of a Jewish homeland.

Their first act of defiance came quickly. On the night of June 16, 1946, every bridge, railroad track, and road that crossed the borders of Palestine was blown up. The act was symbolic, of course. Everything could be rebuilt very quickly. But the Jews had wanted to humiliate the British before the eyes of the world. And they succeeded.

They also infuriated the British. The British government reacted immediately. They would crush this infant rebellion once and for all! On Saturday, June 29, most of the Jewish leaders of Palestine were jailed.

Golda was living alone now—except for a friend who sometimes stayed with her. She and Morris had been living apart for many years. They had finally been forced to face the fact that their natures were just too different to blend into a happy marriage. The children were grown and living lives of their own, too. Ever since he'd been a small boy Menachem had loved music. Now he was studying to be a professional cellist. And Sarah, like Golda so many years before, had been drawn to the life of a kibbutznik. She had left home when she was only seventeen to live on the Kibbutz Revivim, deep in the Negev desert.

So Golda spent much of that tense day alone in her apartment—waiting to be arrested too. "Go into hiding," friends who dropped by begged. "Get out of the country before they come for you too."

Golda refused. "If they want me they know where to find me."

But Golda wasn't arrested. Other women were. But they were not well known like Golda. The British felt that a dirty and crowded prison was not a suitable place for a lady like Golda. Golda was not at all sure she appreciated this "compliment."

But it turned out to be a piece of luck. The British had expected to crush the rebellious Jews. But they only stiffened their determination to fight. Still, they needed a leader. Before long word came from David

Ben-Gurion—who was lucky enough to be out of the country at the time of the raid on Jewish leadership. He chose Golda.

But could she handle this overwhelming new responsibility? Some people thought she couldn't because she was a woman. Some people thought she couldn't because she was *Golda*. For Golda had a reputation for being highly emotional. As one leader said, "In regard to political issues she is strong as iron. But if someone offends her personally, she can begin to cry like a high school girl!" What if she burst into tears at the wrong moment in some conference with the hostile British?

But the people who were closest to Golda were not worried. They knew that her natural dignity would protect her in any real crisis.

They were right. One day Golda was conferring with the British High Commissioner. After a session of hard bargaining she said, "I'm sorry you have to discuss this problem with me, and not one of the leaders who are in jail."

"Oh, you are doing very well, Mrs. Myerson," the High Commissioner said a bit grimly. "Very well."

Golda smiled sweetly.

Another time Golda was discussing the refugee problem with a British official named Ernest Gurney. As always when she discussed this she spoke with great feeling. But Gurney's face remained cold.

Finally he spoke. "Ah, but Mrs. Myerson," he

said, "if Hitler persecuted the Jews so much, surely there must have been some *reason* for it."

Now it was Golda's turn to be cold. She gathered her papers together and rose. "That's how all anti-Semites talk," she said. Then she left the room. From that day on Golda would never meet with that official again.

Golda spent much of her time dealing with the British. But her job was much more than that. She was also deeply involved in the growing rebellion. She helped plan acts of sabotage against the British. She also sent underground fighters out to defend isolated farms and towns against the ever-increasing Arab attacks. On those nights Golda never slept. She knew that probably some of those fighters would not return alive.

"You know what I pray for?" Golda told a friend after such a sleepless night. She pointed to the telephone beside her bed. "I pray for the time when that telephone will ring at night and my heart won't shrink for fear of it being bad news."

Golda also worked with the forces who were trying to bring refugees into Palestine—in spite of the British. "As long as there is still one Jew alive in the world who wants to come and live in the land of Palestine," she said, "the British Government will have to use force if they want to stop him."

That's just what the government was doing. Many ships of the British Navy were patrolling the waters around Palestine. Their only job was to capture shipload after shipload of refugees trying to get in.

One ship was stopped nine miles off shore. It was boarded by soldiers and the captain was ordered to turn around and go back where he came from. The Jews on board went wild with grief! They were so close! They could almost see the Promised Land! Now they were being told they could not enter it.

Twelve of the refugees refused to accept this verdict. In the confusion they jumped overboard and began to swim those nine miles. Eleven of the twelve drowned before they reached Palestine. The last young man was met on the sandy shore of a deserted beach by a watchful patrol and led quickly to safety in a nearby kibbutz.

So 1946 and 1947 were years of deep trouble for Jewish Palestine. They were also years of a growing miracle. The British captured ships full of illegal refugees. And more ships came. They arrested underground fighters. And more appeared to fill their places. Finally there were 100,000 British soldiers in Palestine and still they could not keep order. They couldn't do it! At last the British were forced to admit that they'd had enough. On February 14, 1947, they announced that "His Majesty's Government has decided to refer the whole problem of Palestine to the United Nations."

The United Nations pondered this question for

months. Finally it gave its decision. Palestine would be divided into two independent nations—one Arab and the other Jewish. Statehood would begin in six months' time.

It was going to happen! The dream of a homeland was going to come true! All over Palestine people went wild with joy. Some prayed all night in synagogues. Others danced in the streets. Strangers hugged strangers. Everyone was a friend this night! Again and again people broke into tears of pure joy.

Golda was crying, too. But she didn't even feel the tears rolling down her cheeks. She was standing on a balcony in Jerusalem, watching the joyous scene below. "It's going to happen," she said to a friend standing nearby. After 2,000 years of wandering . . . of persecution . . . of loneliness and longing . . . "It's going to happen!"

But not everyone in Palestine was happy that night. On another balcony, only a few blocks away there was another woman—an Arab. She too watched the crowds celebrating below. "Let them dance," she said coldly. "For soon they will die!"

14

"Murder the Jews!
Murder Them All!"

The United Nations agreement had been worked out very carefully. For six more months the British would remain in the Palestine area. Then, by midnight March 14, 1948, the last of them would be gone. Where Palestine was now the Jewish country of Israel would come into existence. So would a sizable Arab land.

Most people said this agreement was a model of fairness. But the Arabs didn't agree. The Arab nations already had four million square miles in the Middle East. The new Jewish nation would have less than six thousand. But the Arabs wanted this, too.

The day after the United Nations' decision, Golda made a speech. "Our hand is offered to you in peace and friendship," she appealed to the Arabs. But even as she was speaking Arab terrorists killed eight Jews on the road between Haifa and Jerusalem.

That was only the beginning. From then on rioting and terrorism grew with each passing day. But still the Jews held their own. They were able to defend themselves now. Now when they were fighting bands of terrorists. But what would happen when they actually became a nation? Then the Arabs were threatening all-out war.

The Grand Mufti: "Murder the Jews! Murder them all!"

The head of the Moslem Brotherhood: "We will fill the sea with their corpses."

The Secretary General of the Arab League: "This will be a war of extermination, a momentous massacre which will be spoken of like the Mongolian Massacres."

The King of Saudi Arabia: "With fifty million Arabs, what does it matter if we lose ten million people to kill all the Jews?"

An Egyptian newspaper: "Five hundred thousand Iraqis prepare for this holy war. Fifteen thousand Syrians will storm over the Palestine borders and the mighty Egyptian army will throw the Jews into the sea if they dare to declare their nation."

Did the Arabs mean all this? Who could be sure? But Golda summed up the feelings of most of the people when she said, "I suggest you prepare yourselves as if every word were true. And if it should prove to be false we'll survive the disappointment."

But prepare with *what?* The combined forces of five well-equipped, well-trained Arab nations were preparing to pounce on the tiny new nation. Against this the Jews had 60,000 soldiers. But only three thousand of them were really trained. Three thousand soldiers—against hundreds of thousands.

The Arabs were also completely supplied with tanks and airplanes and heavy artillery. The Jews had no heavy equipment at all. They did have a few thousand guns—enough for a fourth of their soldiers. But the guns would soon be useless. They only had ammunition for four days of fighting.

If they were to survive, they must have equipment to fight with. And that meant money. There was only one place where money like that could be gotten—from the Jews of America.

In January 1948 David Ben-Gurion called an emergency meeting of all the political leaders of Jewish Palestine. They had been released from jail after the United Nations had voted for the establishment of the Jewish state. It was a grim session. First Eliezer Kaplan spoke. He had just returned from the United States, and his news wasn't good. He had criss-crossed that land on a fund-raising tour. The tour had not been a success. His audiences had listened to him politely. But most of them had not opened their purses. It wasn't that they didn't care. But they were just so tired of giving. For fifteen years they'd been sending money overseas—ever since the beginning of the Hitler years. Now they felt it was time to start taking care of problems closer to home.

"We need a minimum of twenty-five million dollars to equip the army," Kaplan concluded. "But it is unrealistic to expect it from America. We might eventually raise five million there. That is all."

A dismayed murmur swept around the group. Then suddenly, like a rifle shot, Ben-Gurion's hand came down on the table. "No!" he exploded. "It will *not* be that way. *I* will go to America. *I* will get the money!"

Golda looked at Ben-Gurion's flushed face. And her heart sank. David Ben-Gurion was a unique and very powerful man. A natural leader. But he could also be abrupt to the point of rudeness. And Golda knew how Americans would react to such tactics. He would simply rub them the wrong way—and get nothing at all.

Suddenly Golda found herself on her feet. "Let me go instead," she begged. "What you can do here, I can't. But what you can do in America, perhaps I can too."

Ben-Gurion waved her aside. "*I* am the leader of Palestine," he said. "I must go."

Golda was used to following Ben-Gurion's orders. But now she really surprised herself. "I say we should put it to a vote," she said quietly.

The others at the table were just as aware of Ben-Gurion's short temper. So when the vote was taken it was almost unanimous. Golda Myerson would go to the United States to plead Palestine's case.

Golda didn't even go home to pack a suitcase.

Time was something that must not be wasted now. In only four months the new nation would be declared. In that time money had to be raised. Weapons had to be found, paid for, and shipped to Palestine. So Golda went directly to the Tel-Aviv Airport. The next day she arrived in New York—without even a winter coat.

Suddenly Golda was overcome with panic. It wasn't that she was afraid of speaking in public. But fund-raising was a *profession*—an entire career. People trained for it for years. And now here she was, a total beginner, on the most vital fund-raising mission of all time for the Jews of Palestine. How could she think she'd succeed where real professionals had failed?

But there was nothing to do but go on. Two days later Golda was standing in front of a large audience in the city of Chicago. This was the annual convention of the Council of Jewish Federations. So in the audience were some of the most important—and richest—Jewish leaders in America.

There was little to see of the young woman who had left America in 1921. Her slim figure was now stocky. Her hair was gray and her face lined, her beauty worn away by years of tension and work. But somehow as she stood there the well-dressed, sophisticated audience was very impressed. One man in the audience said later how she affected them all. "We had never seen anyone like her, so plain, so strong, so old-fashioned. Just like a woman out of the Bible."

For a moment Golda gripped the lectern. Then

she began to speak. "Friends, we have no alternative in Palestine. The Mufti and his men have declared war upon us. We have to fight for our lives, for our safety, and for what we have accomplished in Palestine. And perhaps above all, we must fight for Jewish honor and Jewish independence. . . ."

Then Golda told a story. Thirty-five young men— some barely more than children—were trying to reach a town that was being attacked by the Arabs. On the way they were surrounded by a much larger Arab force. They fought brilliantly and desperately, but the odds were too great. "Some of the finest youngsters we have in the country were in that group," Golda said, "and they were all killed. Every one of them." She went on to tell of the last of them. A tale told by an Arab, for there were no more Jews to repeat it. The boy kept fighting until his gun was empty. Then he threw it away and picked up a stone to throw. He died with that stone in his hand.

Golda continued, "I want to say to you, friends, that the Jewish community in Palestine is going to fight to the very end. If we have arms to fight with, we will fight with those. And if not, we will fight with stones in our hands . . .

"I have come here to impress Jews in the United States with the fact that within a very short period, a couple of weeks, we must have in cash between twenty-five and thirty million dollars. In the next two or three weeks we can establish ourselves. . . .

"You cannot decide whether we should fight or not. We will. The Jewish community in Palestine will raise no white flag for the Mufti. That decision is taken. Nobody can change it. You can only decide one thing. Whether we shall be victorious in this fight. That decision American Jews can make. It has to be made quickly—within hours, within days.

"And I beg of you—don't be too late. Don't be bitterly sorry three months from now for what you failed to do today." Golda paused for a moment. Her next words sent a thrill of feeling through her audience. "The time is now."

The speech was over. For a moment the audience sat in total silence. Then suddenly every man and woman in the room rose to cheer Golda—and the vision she had shared with them that day.

They did more than cheer. Before the afternoon was over they had pledged between twenty-five and thirty million dollars! This was more than five times the amount Eliezer Kaplan had said could be expected from *all* the Jews of America. And Golda had raised it in one speech!

This miracle was repeated again and again as she spent the next two and a half months criss-crossing America. She made fund-raising speeches in almost every state. The money continued to pour in. And weapons were bought.

From France, a Jewish agent cabled Golda. He'd found some tanks he wanted to buy. But they would cost ten million dollars. "Buy," she said. Another agent had found a great deal of ammunition. But it would cost another ten million dollars. He sent word that he knew that was too much—so he was returning to Palestine. Golda telegraphed, "Stay."

For two and a half months Golda remained in America. When she returned to Palestine she told a friend, "Well, now I can regard myself as a great *schnorrer*." The two women laughed. For schnorrer was the Yiddish word for beggar.

David Ben-Gurion expressed what Golda had done in a different way. "Someday when our history is written," he said, "it will be said that there was a Jewish woman who got the money which made the nation possible."

It was May 1948 now. In just a few days the new nation of Israel would be declared. Conditions were growing more tense by the minute. Five Arab armies were massing on the borders—ready to pounce on the newborn land. There was only one Arab country that might still be friendly—or at least not an active enemy. This was Trans-Jordan.

King Abdullah of Trans-Jordan had long been a friend of the Jews. After a trip to Palestine in 1946 he wrote, "I was astonished at what I saw of the Jewish settlements. They have colonized the sand dunes, drawn water from them, and transformed them into a paradise."

He was also a personal friend of Golda's. In November 1947—right after the United Nations had declared that Jewish Palestine was to become a nation—he and Golda had held a secret meeting at Naharayim, a small town on the border of Palestine and Jordan. Then Abdullah had been as friendly as ever. He had assured Golda that he would not join in any attack on the Jews.

But lately there had been disturbing rumors reaching the leaders of Jewish Palestine. Rumors that Abdullah was going back on his word. So now Golda asked for another meeting. The chances of anything successful coming from it were slim. But perhaps somehow she could keep him at least neutral.

Abdullah agreed to the meeting. But he sent word that it was now far too dangerous for him to come near the Jewish border. If Golda wanted to talk, *she* would have to come to Amman, the capital of Trans-Jordan.

How could she? Abdullah might be friendly, but Trans-Jordan was an Arab country. Golda was a very well-known Jew. If she were captured there she'd surely be killed.

There was only one way. Golda would have to travel the three hundred miles to Amman disguised as an Arab woman. So during the night of May 10, 1948, Golda and a companion, Ezra Dannin, were driven to the border town of Naharayim. Ezra Dannin was an old friend. He also had special qualifications for this trip. He was an expert on Arab affairs and could speak Arabic like a native.

Now, in Naharayim, Golda and Dannin changed

into long Arab robes. In addition Golda added heavy face veils. But there was one thing she found much harder than she'd thought to disguise. Her walk. So Dannin made her practice. Again and again he made her walk back and forth. "Too much energy! Too much vigor!" he said each time. *"Glide,* Golda, *glide!"*

Finally he told her she could stop. "It'll have to do," he said grudgingly. "With luck you won't be doing much walking anyway." The king had sent a car and driver to carry Golda and Dannin to Amman. Now the really dangerous part of the journey began. "Are you afraid?" Golda asked. Dannin shook his head. "I've been close to death too many times. It has made me a fatalist."

What a trip that was! War was due to break out in only four days. Trans-Jordan was on full military alert. There were military checkpoints everywhere. Again and again they were stopped and their papers examined. Dannin did all the talking. He pretended to be a rich Arab merchant traveling with his wife. Golda sat huddled in a corner of the back seat, trying to look as meek and shy as she could.

Finally—after being stopped ten times—Golda and Dannin arrived in Amman. They went to the home of a trusted friend of the king. After a few minutes the king himself arrived.

He was friendly enough. But Golda could tell he was ill at ease. As politely as she could she reminded him of the promise of friendship he'd made in November.

He made no effort to deny it. But now he shook his head sadly. "Then I was alone," he said. "Now I am one of five. I have no choice and I cannot act otherwise." Because the other Arab nations were so powerful, he felt he *had* to ally with them.

But the king did have an idea. Why not postpone declaring the new nation in Palestine? If the Jews did this, he was sure he could convince the other Arab leaders to withdraw their armies. By such a simple move, war could be avoided. "After all," he concluded, "I do not understand why the Jews should be in such a hurry to declare a state."

Golda managed to control her temper. "A people who have waited two thousand years can hardly be described as being in a hurry," she said quietly.

Now Golda and the king looked at each other. They were both sad. They were still friends. But they were separated by something too powerful for individual people—the politics of nations.

The meeting had been a failure. It was time to go. "Perhaps we shall meet again after the war, when there will be a Jewish state," Golda said in parting.

"Perhaps," Abdullah said sadly. For a moment more they gazed at each other. Then the king turned and was gone.

The trip to Amman hadn't been fun. The trip back was a nightmare. Their car was stopped for identification checks again and again. And by now their Arab driver knew who they were. At each checkpoint he became more nervous. Finally he began to mutter to himself in Arabic.

"What's he saying?" Golda asked Dannin.

"You don't want to know," he said grimly.

Finally the driver's panic became too great. He knew if he was caught with these Jews he would die. He jammed on the brakes and said something savagely to Dannin.

Dannin answered just as savagely. But the driver shook his head.

"Hell!" Dannin exploded.

"What *is* it?" Golda demanded to know.

"He says he's had enough," Dannin said between clenched teeth. "He says we have to get out and walk from here—no matter what the king's orders are."

"But he can't do that!" Golda cried. "We're still in Jordan! We'll be killed."

"He says the border is only a few miles ahead. According to him, we'll make it in an hour."

There was nothing else to do. Golda and Dannin got out of the car and began to walk. Luckily there was no moon. But the black night seemed to press down on them like a suffocating rug.

"Dannin," Golda whispered, after they'd walked for a while. "Do you think he was telling the truth—about the border being so close?"

"I don't know."

They stumbled on in silence.

"Dannin," Golda whispered again.

"Yes, Golda?"

"Do you remember my asking if you were scared?"

"Yes."

"Well, I admit it. *I* am now!"

All around them there were small night sounds. Were they the sounds of animals and birds and the rising wind—or were they Arab border patrols?

If they were caught there would be no escape from this. Decent Arab ladies simply didn't take late-night walks in the Jordanian hills.

The minutes seemed to stretch like hours. Surely they should have come to the border before this! Finally Golda whispered, "Do you see what I see?"

Again Dannin answered "Yes." In the east the sky was just a little less black. Soon it would be day. And the game would be up.

Suddenly they froze. There had been a sound. Something like a twig breaking. Like a foot kicking a small stone . . . Dannin's hand gripped Golda's arm. *Don't move,* she knew it meant.

Now the sounds were louder, closer. They could make out the figure of a man—which meant he could see them, too. Dannin decided to bluff it out. "Who goes there?" he said in Arabic.

But the answer was in Hebrew! It was a Jewish scout who'd been sent to find them when they hadn't returned at the proper time. "Give me your hands," he said softly. "I'll lead you to the border." Golda grasped that calloused hand tightly—and knew she'd never felt anything quite so wonderful in her entire life.

It was almost four o'clock in the afternoon of May 14, 1948. Golda was sitting with thirty-seven other leaders of Jewish Palestine at a long T-shaped table in the Tel-Aviv Art Museum. In the audience there were nearly two hundred more people. The room was packed. But a strange almost-silence hung over everything. For this was the day of days! In just a few minutes ceremonies would begin for "the establishment of the Jewish State in Palestine called Israel."

Israel. Golda said the word to herself. *Israel.* For centuries that word had been just a word in songs, a part of prayers, a longing in people's hearts. Now it would be printed on the maps of the world. After 2,000 years Israel lived again!

It was four o'clock. David Ben-Gurion rose and adjusted the microphone before him. In his hands he held the Proclamation of Independence. Golda smiled as she looked at the man who would soon be Prime Minister of Israel. "I bet his wife had a hard time getting him into *that,*" she thought. For Ben-Gurion was dressed in a sober dark blue business suit— and a tie. Everyone in Palestine knew how much their fiery leader hated such clothes. *His* idea of a really proper outfit was a worker's cotton shirt and pants.

Now, with one final tug at his tie, Ben-Gurion began to speak. "The Land of Israel was the birthplace of the Jewish people. Here their spiritual, religious and national identity was formed. Here they achieved independence and created a culture of national and universal significance. Here they wrote and gave the Bible to the world.

"Exiled from the Land of Israel, the Jewish people remained faithful to it in all the centuries of . . ."

Golda continued to hear the words. But suddenly her mind was flooded with memories, too. She remembered a frightened little girl in Russia, crouching in the mud as Cossacks' horses jumped within inches over her head. She remembered that same little girl getting her head knocked by a drunken peasant. To this day she remembered that peasant's words. "That's what we'll do with all Jews! Then we'll be rid of them!"

And there were good memories, too. Memories of her growing years in America. Memories of friendships . . . And school . . . Golda remembered learning about the American Declaration of Independence— declaring freedom and the rights of man. Now, in just a few minutes, she too would be signing just such a document—for the state of Israel. At this thought a shiver of pure feeling swept through her. And, as usual when she was deeply moved, tears filled her eyes.

But Golda blinked them back. She remembered life on the kibbutz—and how happy she'd been. She remembered Morris, and the troubles they'd had. Dear

Morris. Although for years now they had lived apart, they still shared a very real affection. Golda remembered the dark years of Hitler. And the struggles for statehood.

And now . . . Now a country was about to be born! "In my own time," Golda whispered. "In my own time." No longer could she hold back the tears.

Golda felt a hand close over hers. It was Moshe Shertok. He was handing her a pen. Golda took it. And with the tears still streaming down her face, she signed her name to the Proclamation of Independence of the new state of Israel.

15

"Golda Shelanu" — Our Golda

One day after Israel became a nation the Arabs made good their threats. The combined forces of five Arab armies attacked the tiny land. Lebanon and Syria swept down from the north. Trans-Jordan and Iraq pushed in from the east. Egypt advanced from the south.

The war would be over in ten days, a military expert from England said. The Jews simply couldn't hold out any longer than that. Other military experts agreed—except they thought the war would be over in even less time.

The Arabs were confident, too. They were so confident that they even had a timetable of destruction. According to this schedule the city of Haifa was to fall on May 20. Tel-Aviv and Jerusalem would fall by the 25th.

But how the Jews fought! They were outmanned, outweaponed, outtrained. The only thing they soon proved was that they weren't outclassed.

In the north soldiers were driving back the armies of Syria and Lebanon. To the south Egypt was stalled by the fighting kibbutzniks of the Negev settlements. Even the people of Jerusalem—who were cut off and growing hungrier every day—refused to surrender.

"It's a *ness*," people were saying. A miracle. Or as one old man exclaimed to his son, "I must be a saint. If I were not, I would not have lived to see this day."

Weapons were pouring into the country now— many of them bought with the dollars that Golda had raised in America. But more weapons were needed desperately. Three days after the war began David Ben-Gurion summoned Golda to his office in Tel-Aviv.

"Sit down, Golda," he said wearily. "You must be tired."

"Not as tired as you," Golda replied.

"Ummm . . . Yes, yes . . . ," Ben-Gurion muttered distractedly, pawing through some papers on his desk. Finally he found what he was looking for. He held up a stack of telegraph forms. "They're from America," he said.

Golda knew what was coming. She'd been getting telegrams, too. Americans, Jews and non-Jews alike, were at a fever pitch of sympathy because of the Arab attacks. Just a few months before, Golda had toured the country and raised more than fifty million dollars. Now, these telegrams were saying there was much more money for Israel. If only Golda would come again.

But she didn't want to! Not now! Not when Israel was only four days old—and in the midst of a life-and-death war! But Ben-Gurion just looked at her. "You know how much we need that money," he said.

And Golda knew. So once more she stifled her personal desires. "All right," she said. "Have you got someone who can drive me to the airport?"

Golda landed at New York City's La Guardia Airport. A few minutes later she started through customs, and the agent asked her to open her purse. "It's only routine, ma'am," he said politely.

But a perplexed expression soon settled on his face as he began to pull out a very long, very gauzy piece of material.

"What's this?" he asked.

Golda felt her face growing red. "Well . . . ," she answered, "it's a veil."

"A *veil?*" He looked at Golda hard—and she knew just what he was thinking. What would a nice Jewish lady want with a long, fancy veil?

How could she explain to this American that only eight days before she had worn that veil as she traveled deep into enemy territory to talk to an Arab king? Or that—still shaky with fear from an unexpected night-time walk through the Trans-Jordan hills—she had absentmindedly stuffed it into her purse? And that in the incredible turmoil and confusion of a country newly born and suddenly at war, she just had never thought to take it out?

Finally Golda took the veil from the puzzled man. She stuffed it back in her purse, grinned, shrugged, and walked on.

Golda expected to be in the United States for about a month. But as she was preparing to go home, she received a message from Ben-Gurion. He wanted her to undertake another job. He wanted her to represent Israel as its first minister to Moscow.

No! Everything in Golda rebelled! *This* she would not do! The war was still going on. Her son was in the army. Her daughter was on a kibbutz that was even now under Egyptian attack. Surely her place was in Israel, not some foreign country!

But as usual, after a period of inner rebellion, Golda did what was asked of her. She returned to Israel to pick a staff. On September 3, 1948, the Israeli delegation arrived in Moscow. Soon Golda began to function as Madame Minister to Russia.

There were many meetings and conferences and formal parties to attend. And every Friday evening the Israeli Embassy held an open house. They did not serve liquor or fancy food—that cost too much. But word soon got around anyway. There was fun to be had at the Israeli Embassy—more fun than at any other place in town.

So all sorts of people came to those Friday Nights. Important diplomats, members of the delegations of other nations, reporters, businessmen, actors, and artists. There was only one group that was never there. Russian Jews.

"When we set out for Moscow," Golda said later, "we wondered . . . No, we doubted whether under such a regime with its power and cruelty, any trace of the Jewish people remained." For the Communist government of Russia was a rigid dictatorship. They disliked minorities of all kinds. They also distrusted religion. So from the time they came to power the Jews of Russia had been told to forget their Jewishness. If they did not, life would be made miserable for them.

There were said to be three million Jews still left in Russia. But no one knew for sure. So few still practiced their faith openly—and these were mostly old men and women.

The Israelis were not very religious. But still Golda felt that they should show their concern for this group. "It is fitting that we join whomever is left," she said.

So one Saturday soon after they arrived, the Israelis set out on foot for the one synagogue in the city that had remained open.

There were supposed to be five hundred thousand Jews in Moscow alone. But that September Saturday only three hundred worshipers were in the synagogue. Few of them were young. "An old man's religion," Golda mourned.

In Orthodox synagogues women sit separately

from the men. So now Golda and the other Israeli women moved off to sit in the balcony—which was also almost empty. No one knew they were there except the rabbi. So step by step the regular service progressed. Then, right at the end, his eyes shining with emotion, the rabbi announced, "I would like now to offer a prayer for our Minister from the State of Israel, Mrs. Golda Myerson."

An emotion almost like an electric shock passed through the congregation. Everyone exclaimed with surprise and twisted in his seat to look up at Golda in the balcony. While the rabbi prayed, many of them began to weep openly.

As Golda and the others left the synagogue the old people swarmed around her. Finally the crowd became so thick she was separated from the rest of her party. That didn't matter, Golda decided. The hotel where the Israelis were staying was only a few blocks from the synagogue. She'd find her way back alone.

But soon she realized she was lost. Just then an old man appeared by her side. "Don't talk to me," he said under his breath in Yiddish. "I'll walk ahead, and you follow."

When they were in sight of the hotel he turned and in a voice thick with emotion whispered the age-old Hebrew blessing: "Blessed are we that we have lived to see this day." Then, before Golda could thank him, he was gone.

For the next few weeks Golda and the others

stayed away from the synagogue. They knew that the Russian government might become angry and cause trouble if they went too often. But then it was Rosh Hashanah—the celebration of the Jewish New Year. "Of course we must go now," Golda said. "But so as not to cause trouble, we will not announce that we're going."

On the first day of Rosh Hashanah, Golda and the others quietly left the hotel. And once more they set out for the synagogue on foot. Before they had gone very far they noticed that the streets were crowded with people. As they neared the synagogue the crowds grew even thicker. There were young people and old, and many children, too. There were even some young men in Soviet Army uniforms. And what a happy crowd it was. What could it be? A parade coming, perhaps? Or some kind of Russian holiday?

Then Golda saw all the *yarmulkas*—skullcaps—and the prayer shawls. And she knew. They were Jews! All Jews! Thousands of them! Later the figure would be set at close to fifty thousand.

Now she could hear what they were saying. "Shana Tova, Goldele! Shana Tova!" *Happy New Year, Golda!*

"And it was all for you, Goldie," someone said later. But Golda shook her head. "It was for Israel. If an Israeli broomstick had appeared in their midst, those Russian Jews would have hugged it!"

Golda was swept along by the crowd until she

reached the synagogue. There she was escorted up to the women's section. A section that was packed this time!

All during the service women kept coming up to her. Some wanted to ask whispered questions about relatives in Israel. Others simply reached out and touched her hand or the sleeve of her dress.

After the services Golda was once more engulfed by the crowds outside. Other Russians watching this shook their heads in puzzlement. "What's going on?" they asked again and again. And again and again Golda heard the Jews explain to their Christian neighbors. "Eto nasha Golda." *It's our Golda.*

It was a holy day—and on such a day a good Jew does not ride in a vehicle of any kind. But the crowd was growing more excited by the moment. Some of Golda's staff began to fear that she might be hurt. They found a taxi and slipped her inside. "And for God's sake, Golda, stay there!" one of them snapped. They knew she was perfectly capable of popping right back out again.

Golda did roll down the window and lean out. It was plain that she was trying to say something. But at first the noise of the crowd drowned her out. Slowly they fell silent. And in Yiddish—that universal folk language of the Jews—Golda said, "A dank eich wos ihr geblieben Yiden." *I thank you that you have remained Jews.*

In February 1949, the United Nations helped negotiate a truce between Israel and the Arab nations. The toll had been great. But the war was over! Now the country was finally free to work on peacetime challenges and problems.

Oh, how Golda longed to be there! "I want to do something *real*," she grumbled again and again. Madame Minister to Russia was thoroughly bored with parties and meetings and all the other fancy trappings of high-level diplomacy.

Several months later Golda got her wish. A telegram arrived from Prime Minister David Ben-Gurion, asking Golda to become Israel's first Minister of Labor.

Now this was a job she could really get her teeth into! For as Minister of Labor it would be Golda's responsibility to see to the welfare of every new immigrant arriving in the country.

And they were arriving at a rate of nearly a thousand a day! They came from seventy-two different countries. They spoke dozens of different languages. Some wore modern clothes. Others seemed to have stepped straight out of Biblical times. There were the sad-faced ones bearing the physical and emotional scars of the concentration camps. Others were fleeing from hostile Arab lands. There were Turkish Jews and Afghanistani Jews, Jews from Austria and Jews from Abyssinia. There were dark-skinned Jews from Libya. And Jews from China. There were Jews who spoke

Aramaic—the language of Jesus. And Jews from India clad in bright-colored saris.

A few brought money and skills. But most were desperately poor. And by Western standards, hopelessly ignorant. One group of Jews arrived from Yemen. They were taken to one of the tent cities where they would live until homes could be built for them. Inside the tents were cots for them to sleep on. The next morning they were found sleeping under the cots instead. They thought the cots were some kind of protection against an unknown danger. They were issued knives and forks and spoons. The Yemenites stared at them in puzzlement. They'd never seen eating utensils before.

It was Golda's job to take these people and turn them into productive citizens of Israel. She gloried in the task. "They call America a melting pot!" she exulted. "People should see what's happening here!"

Not everyone was so happy. "We just can't absorb this many people," some said. "Especially the ones that don't know how to do *anything!*"

"They'll learn on the job," Golda answered.

"What job?"

"We'll make jobs," she said.

And she did. The new immigrants built their own homes—and some became carpenters. They built roads—and some became construction workers and engineers. In a few years they would learn how to be farmers and factory workers, teachers and businessmen and airline pilots.

But in the meantime this "ingathering of the immigrants" was costing a great deal of money. Most Israelis were willing to pay it somehow. But a few grumbled. As one man said, when he was told his taxes would soon be raised again, "Two thousand years we waited for our nation to be reborn—and it had to happen to me!"

Perhaps immigration should be slowed down, just for a few years. Just until Israel was economically stronger. This kind of talk infuriated Golda. For wasn't unlimited immigration what Israel was all about? Hadn't the dream all along been to make a place where *all* Jews could come—old and young, well and sick, wealthy and desperately poor?

"Look at the facts, Golda," she was told. "Look at the figures . . ." But Golda as usual was busy looking at people. "Let's have *more* problems with absorption of Jews," she replied to her critics. "If anybody knows in the first place what it means to be a refugee and in the second place how to solve a refugee problem, then we are tops. After all, we *are* a refugee people."

And so the amazing immigration continued. By 1959 almost a million immigrants had entered Israel. Hundreds of towns and agricultural villages had been established. Water had been brought to many new areas of the desert. Tens of thousands of men and women had been trained for new jobs. Wide roads now stretched across the land. *Goldene Wegen*—golden roads—the Israelis called them, after Golda, who had somehow found the money to build them.

Golda was Minister of Labor for seven years. "The most beautiful years," she said many times. But then Ben-Gurion asked her to take another job. He asked her to become Foreign Minister of Israel. This was the second most important job in the land!

"What an honor!" a friend said.

"I know," Golda answered glumly. She would have been happy to remain Labor Minister for the rest of her life. Besides, there were so many things about being Foreign Minister that she didn't like.

Golda would have to spend her time dealing with diplomats and political problems. She would have to move from her comfortable apartment into an official mansion—a great cold place filled with uncomfortable formal furniture.

She'd have to change her name, too. For years David Ben-Gurion had been trying to get Israelis to adopt Hebrew last names. He said their old names were like tags—tying them to old lands and lives. But for years Golda had resisted. She was perfectly happy with the name Myerson. Now Ben-Gurion really insisted. If Golda was going to represent Israel before the rest of the world, she *must* have a Hebrew name. Finally Golda gave in. But she was determined to choose a name that was as close to Myerson as possible. Finally she chose Meir—which in Hebrew means "illuminate."

Golda was a very popular Foreign Minister. She

was so naturally diplomatic and kind. But she could be blunt, too. In 1964 Golda represented Israel at the Independence Day ceremonies for the new African nation of Zambia. One day the neighboring country of South Rhodesia invited all the diplomats there to cross over the border and view Victoria Falls—the highest waterfall in the world.

They were met at the border by policemen who asked them to line up in two separate lines. One for white people and one for black. In Southern Rhodesia, they were informed, they would have to travel on segregated buses.

Golda immediately said, "No, thank you, I can do without the Falls." She turned and started back to her car. About halfway there she heard a commotion behind her. She turned to see all the dignitaries streaming after her—even the ones who had been lining up a few moments before.

Golda was an excellent Foreign Minister— primarily perhaps because she cared so much for her fellow human beings. As she said in a speech before the United Nations, the world's great problems might be closer to solution if more political leaders allowed themselves to "feel more and think less."

There was only one aspect of being Foreign Minister that gave Golda trouble. That was all the formality associated with the job. Golda just couldn't help being Golda. And there was nothing formal about that!

Once she was staying in a New York hotel. A

woman on her staff knocked on her door. "Come in," Golda called. "I'm in the bathroom washing out a few things."

The woman was horrified. "But you're the Foreign Minister of Israel!" she blurted out.

"I'm also *me*," Golda replied tartly—and went on scrubbing.

Another time she was on a plane from Israel to the United States. The Foreign Minister of France happened to be on the plane, too. He was riding first class of course—as important people do. Golda, who never tried to act important, was riding tourist class. Besides, it was cheaper that way.

The French Foreign Minister was told she was on board, and went back to talk with her. Golda never forgot the shocked look on his face when he saw her squeezed in between two fat American tourists.

Because she was Foreign Minister she had a full staff of servants—a cook, a chauffeur, a maid, and a housekeeper. But Golda never treated them like servants. When she was not entertaining dignitaries at formal dinners, they always sat down to eat with her.

One day Golda began to laugh. She pointed to Yehudith, the housekeeper. "You come from Germany, right? And Esther comes from Iraq. And Itzhak . . . ," Golda smiled at the shy young chauffeur, "he is from Romania. While I—I come from Russia, by way of America. Quite a regular United Nations we have here around this table!"

would be better than Golda Meir, the most beloved person in Israel?

But once more some Israelis wondered if Golda could manage this job—even for a few months. After all, she had been sick a lot lately. She still had a reputation for being too emotional. She was a woman. And most of all, she was too old.

"Seventy is no sin!" Golda said. "Of course," she added, "it's no great honor, either."

The Arabs, too, didn't expect much of Golda. They called her *Golda Lox*. They said she was like a broken-down horse—unable to pull even the lightest wagon-load of state problems.

That was before they had dealt with her. A few months later an Arab leader was asked what he thought of Prime Minister Meir now. "She's hard as nails!" he snapped.

Golda hadn't wanted to be Prime Minister. But now she surprised everyone—including herself. She'd expected to serve for a few months and then step aside for someone more suitable. Instead, she served five years! For soon it became plain to the people of Israel—and the rest of the world—that Golda was a natural born Head of State. She could work long hours without tiring. She was able to keep the many strong personalities in her government working together. She had a reputation for absolute honesty. "Golda is the only politician I know," a co-worker said, "who says the same thing in public that she says in private."

Most of all she was tough.

And the Prime Minister of Israel had to be tough. More than twenty-one years had passed since Israel became a nation. And still the Arab countries refused to accept her existence. In 1948 the Arabs had attacked Israel from three sides. In 1956 and 1967 they once more massed along Israel's borders—in even greater numbers and with much more powerful weapons and equipment. Again and again Egypt's Radio Cairo blared the same message: "The day of Israel's destruction approaches. This is our decision and this is our faith. There shall be no peace . . . for we demand vengeance—and vengeance means death to Israel." During one of those tense pre-war days the President of Iraq put the Arab goal even more simply. "The clear aim is to wipe Israel off the map," he said. And over and over again the Arabs sent a warning to Israel's one-eyed General Moshe Dayan: "We are coming to put out your other eye."

In both 1956 and 1967 Israel was ringed by hostile enemies. If these enemies struck the first blow the country would almost certainly be destroyed. So the Israelis did the only thing they could. They leapt out of the fast-closing traps. They struck the first blows in each war instead.

This upset many people in other parts of the world. They said that Israel had been wrong to attack first—that this made her an aggressor nation. But the Israelis knew they had no choice. As Golda soberly pointed out, "If we have to choose between being dead and pitied, and being alive with a bad image, we'd rather be alive and have the bad image.''

But perhaps the Arabs had not meant to attack. This is what they announced loudly after each war. Perhaps they were just trying to keep things tense.

Whenever people suggested this to Golda, she spoke of something that had happened during the 1956 war. A number of Egyptian officers were captured. Among their papers the Israeli soldiers found one that was particularly interesting. ''Every commander is to prepare himself and his subordinates for the inevitable campaign against Israel,'' the paper stated, ''for the purpose of fulfilling our exalted aim, which is to annihilate Israel and bring about her destruction in the shortest possible time in the most brutal and savage battles.''

16

The Yom Kippur War

The October air was cool and dry, a perfect night for sleeping. But for hours Golda lay awake, staring into the dark. Something was wrong—she just knew it. Something was terribly wrong.

It was almost 4 A.M. before Golda finally managed to fall asleep. Minutes later the phone beside her bed shrilled—and she was instantly awake once more.

"Golda!" Her military aide's voice was edged with panic. "We've just received absolute confirmation: It's going to happen. Egypt and Syria are going to attack at 6 P.M. today!"

War! Another all-out Arab effort to erase Israel from the map! For a few stunned moments the only thing Golda could think was, "How could this happen?"

Three times before Israel's hostile neighbors had plunged the tiny nation into war. Three times before Israel had fought against overwhelming odds to win amazing victories. But this time there was one terrible difference. Surprise.

Israel had one of the finest military intelligence services in the world. Always before the country had known days and even weeks ahead just where and when the enemy planned to attack. So they'd had time to mobilize—to get men and equipment to their units and all units into the best positions for the coming battles. Now they didn't have weeks or even days. They had only a few hours.

There had been hints of trouble. As early as May Israeli Intelligence had received reports that both Syria and Egypt were building up their troop strength along their borders with Israel.

Golda read these reports and called a special meeting of her three top military advisors. "What if this is the first step toward another war?" she asked them. But they refused to be concerned.

"It's just training maneuvers," her head of intelligence soothed.

Then in September more disturbing reports filtered in. The Syrians were once again increasing their troop strength along their side of the Golan Heights—that thin line of low hills which was Israel's only protection to the north.

Golda called another emergency meeting. But still

her advisors would not worry. "Oh, the Syrians are always bluffing," her minister of defense said.

Then, only yesterday, Golda had received a piece of information that upset her badly. There were many Russians working in Syria. Now they and their families were all packing up and leaving the country.

"Why the haste?" Golda asked. "What do those Russians know that we don't? Maybe we should issue at least a partial call-up."

Even now her advisors did not change their opinion. They reminded her how much such a massive military call-up would cost. "Remember, we did it last year—and all for nothing," her chief of staff said.

Golda nodded. But to herself she thought, "Maybe that's *why* nothing happened."

Finally the meeting was over. The men filed out of Golda's office. Then the head of intelligence stuck his head back around the door. "Golda," he said kindly, "you can be assured we would get adequate warning of any real trouble brewing. So don't worry. There won't be a war."

But Golda did worry. She just couldn't get those Russians out of her mind. Finally she gave herself a shake. She would just have to trust the judgment of her advisors. After all, they weren't ordinary soldiers. They were all experienced generals—men at the very top of their professions.

It was little wonder that when she got that 4 A.M. phone call, Golda could only ask, "How could this happen?'' But now was no time for searching questions. Now was a time for action. Quickly Golda threw on some clothes and headed for her office in downtown Tel-Aviv.

As her car sped through the streets she saw an old man and a little boy, walking along hand in hand. The old man had a prayer shawl over his shoulder. Golda knew exactly where they were going. To some nearby synagogue. For today, October 6, 1973, was Yom Kippur—the most solemn and sacred day of the Jewish religious calendar.

Yom Kippur is a day unlike any other for Jews everywhere. All over the world religious Jews fast. They stay home from work and spend the day in synagogues, praying for forgiveness for any wrongdoing they might have committed in the past year.

On this day in Israel everything would come to a standstill. No newspapers would be published. No television or radio would be broadcast. There would be no public transportation. All schools, shops, restaurants, and offices would be closed. Worst of all, most of Israel's soldiers had been given leave, to be home with their families.

Golda knew that mobilization was an extremely difficult task at any time. Today it would be almost impossible. But it would have to be done—and in the shortest time possible. That would be only a part of Golda's job in the next few days as she strived to lead Israel safely through the most dangerous time it had ever known. Later she referred to those days as a nightmare. And they were.

Israel, unprepared, faced not one, but two gigantic war machines. Between them Syria and Egypt had twice as many tanks and planes as Israel. They had three times as many combat-ready soldiers. And four times as many heavy artillery pieces.

Around the clock news poured in from both fronts—all of it bad. By the end of the first day 30,000 Egyptian troops had crossed the Suez Canal into the Israeli-occupied Sinai Desert. In the beginning there were only 436 Israeli soldiers facing them to stem the flood. They fought like wild men. But the odds were far too great. The Egyptians pushed steadily forward.

At least the Israelis in the south had space to fall back. The Egyptians would have to cross more than a hundred miles of empty desert before they came to the first Israeli settlements.

But in the north only one thing separated Israel from certain destruction—the Golan Heights. If the Syrians managed to take these hills nothing could stop them. They would sweep down like a tidal wave into the very heart of Israel.

Once more the odds against Israel were staggering. All along the heights fierce battles were breaking out as Syrian tanks and armored vehicles battered the pitifully thin Israeli forward line. But somehow, hour after hour, that line held.

Near the center of the heights Colonel Avigdor Janos and his Seventh Armored Brigade were in the midst of the heaviest fighting. Like every Israeli commander, he was badly outnumbered—both in men and equipment. But how his men fought. As dawn broke on the second day of war they counted 130 disabled Syrian tanks and more than twice that number of other heavy equipment.

This was a staggering loss, but the Syrians could afford it. For years their every military need had been filled by Russia. Now they just moved up new tanks and continued the attack.

All through that second day Janos and his ragged unit managed to hold on. But he knew it was only a matter of time now. Almost all his tanks were damaged or destroyed. Almost every one of his tank commanders was either wounded or dead.

Late in the afternoon the Syrians launched the heaviest attack yet. They hammered away at the exhausted Israelis with heavy artillery fire. Then though the thick smoke came row after row of Syrian tanks. There were hundreds of them!

Colonel Janos had only six tanks in fighting condition. Six—against hundreds. It was time to send the message every leader hates above all others. He must inform his commanding officer, General Rafel Eytan, that there was no longer any choice. He had to retreat.

General Eytan quickly sent back a reply. ''Just hold for half an hour more.'' Somehow Janos did. And it was during those few desperate last minutes, he said later, that the miracle began to happen.

Suddenly he heard a single Israeli tank rumbling up

the hill behind him. A few minutes later another arrived. And then another. He and his men had held out alone for two terrifying days. Now finally reinforcements were reaching the front lines.

The odds were still terribly lopsided. But Janos never hesitated. And his men fought as if each had personally adopted as his own Golda's favorite expression: "Ein lanu derech acheret." *We have no alternative.*

The battle raged for hours. For every Israeli tank hit, ten Syrian tanks were destroyed. Sometimes more. Then suddenly the terrible noise of shelling began to fade. "Look at that!" one of the Israeli officers shouted. "Just look at that!"

The Syrians were retreating! Their tanks were turning in their tracks and rumbling back to Syria! They had started with every advantage. More troops. Vastly superior equipment. And perhaps the biggest advantage of all—surprise. And still they had been beaten back by a handful of exhausted young men in a few battered tanks. It was a true miracle—a miracle of human spirit.

A few minutes later General Eytan sent a second message to Colonel Janos. "You have saved the people of Israel."

Israeli troops were fighting with the same naked courage on the Egyptian front. After an agonizing week of holding actions and slow retreats, the Israeli army was finally up to full strength. Now, fifteen miles into the Sinai Desert, another giant tank battle was about to begin.

For the first time both sides were almost evenly matched. The Egyptians moved up 500 tanks. Almost as many Israeli tanks were waiting for them. The battle began at dawn. And it was another bloodbath—this time for the Egyptians.

With pinpoint accuracy the Israeli gunners blew up tank after tank. Before noon over 250 Arab tanks had been destroyed. More than half!

At this point Egyptian morale crumbled, and the remaining tanks began to flee toward the Suez Canal and safety. But the Israelis were not finished. They followed behind and managed to knock out another fifty-five enemy tanks—without losing a single one of their own.

That evening Golda received a telephone call from her chief of staff, David Elezar. Golda could tell he was exhausted, but his voice was filled with deep pride. "Golda, it's going to be all right. We are back to being ourselves—and they are back to being themselves."

"I knew that bloody battles lay ahead," Golda said later. "But when I heard those words I also knew that the tide had turned."

On October 22 the United Nations called for a cease-fire. The war was over at last. By any military analysis the Israelis had won the most striking victory in their history of victories.

But there was no rejoicing in Israel. The price had been so terribly high. Many Israeli citizens felt it had been too high. They blamed their leaders for being unprepared.

Golda agreed with them. "Oh, I know all my expert advisors said there would be no war. But I should have listened to the warnings of my own heart and ordered a call-up. I will never forgive myself for that one decision I failed to make, and I shall live with that terrible knowledge for the rest of my life." Then she would often add softly, "I will never again be the same woman I was before the Yom Kippur War."

Just after the war Golda showed a visitor a large leather-bound book that was always kept in the Prime Minister's office. In it was the photograph and biography of every boy who had ever died in any of Israel's wars. "So many pages will have to be added now," Golda said sadly.

But it was not just dead Israelis who saddened Golda. Once a reporter asked if she had ever killed anyone. "No," Golda answered, "but I don't console myself for it. There's no difference between killing and making decisions by which you send others to kill. It's exactly the same thing. And maybe it's worse."

Now Golda spoke very slowly, as if the words filled her with great weariness. "You know, the Arabs' greatest sin is not making war against Israel and killing her sons. We can forgive them for that. Their greatest sin is that they made *us* kill them. That they made us teach our boys how to kill."

Golda had so many reasons for being sad in those months following the Yom Kippur War. One that upset her most of all was that not one democratic country in

Europe had helped Israel in any way during the war. Not long after, Golda spoke of this at an international conference of world leaders.

She was a deeply respected person. So as she rose to speak a deep hush fell over the room. As always, Golda spoke with great simplicity. First she told how Israel had been taken by surprise, how they had been fooled by their own wishful thinking into believing the Arabs wouldn't attack. She explained how it had been touch and go for so many days, and what a price they had finally been forced to pay to win the war.

Golda paused and took a deep breath before she went on. "I just want to understand, in light of this, what it is really about today. Here you are, all of you. We are all old comrades, long-standing friends. So what did you think? On what grounds did you make your decisions?"

When Golda was done, the chairman of the meeting rose to ask if anyone else wanted to speak. Nobody did. The silence grew heavier and heavier. Then someone behind Golda—she never knew who it was—said very clearly, "Of course they can't talk. Their throats are choked with oil."

The lure of Arab oil. No one needed to speak now. It had all been said—by a man whose face Golda never saw.

Golda was so tired. "You know," she confided to a friend, "sometimes it seems to me that everything that has happened since the afternoon of October 6 has happened on one endless day.'' More than anything Golda wanted that day to end.

Finally she came to a decision. ''This is it,'' she told herself. ''There is a limit to what I can take, and I have now reached that limit.'' On June 4, 1974, Prime Minister Golda Meir retired.

A new government came to power. Not just a new government—a new generation as well. For Golda had been the last of the pioneers, the last of the builders and dreamers who had come so long ago to take a barren stretch of sand and turn it into a nation.

Now it was time for the sabras—the native born—to take over. Yitzhak Rabin, the new Prime Minister, had been born in Jerusalem the year Morris and Golda arrived in Palestine. Golda knew his style would be very different from hers. She also knew that one basic thing would always remain the same, for these younger men and women understood the most essential thing of all. ''Like me, they know that for the Jewish people to remain a people, there must be a Jewish State where Jews can live as Jews—never again on sufferance and never again as a minority.''

17

The Last Years

Golda knew how many lives had been lost because Israel had not been prepared for war. And she blamed herself for it. Most Israelis were not nearly so harsh. One day a group of soldiers brought her a special present. It was a blue and white Star of David they had knitted while they'd been prisoners of war in Egypt. "It served us as a sort of flag," one of the young men explained. "We would like you to have it now."

Golda was deeply touched. She'd been a world leader for so many years. During those years she had received a great number of presents—some quite rare and beautiful, others of great historic or monetary value. But this slightly dirty and not quite perfectly shaped Star of David had a value none of them could ever equal. Golda framed it and hung it in a special spot of honor on her living room wall.

She also received many letters from people all over the land. Some were from parents of boys who had died in battle. Others were from young soldiers still lying wounded in hospitals. The same simple thread of support ran through them all: "Be well. Be strong. Everything will be all right."

Golda was no longer a part of the government. But her popularity and influence continued to reach far beyond the borders of Israel. For longer than she cared to remember she had been one of Israel's foremost public speakers in foreign lands. Now she was a private citizen. But the invitations still poured in. And Golda continued to fulfill as many of these requests as she could—because she felt it was her responsibility to help explain Israel to the world.

She spoke about Israel's special need always to be prepared: "Many people have lost wars, true. And many people's countries have been occupied by foreign powers. Our history is much more tragic. Hitler took care of six million Jews. If we lose a war, that's the end forever. If one fails to understand this, then one fails to understand our obstinacy."

She spoke about war: "War is an immense stupidity. I'm sure that someday children in school will study the history of the men who made war as you study an absurdity. They'll be astonished, they'll be shocked, just as today we're shocked by cannibalism."

She spoke about peace: "We say peace and the echo comes back war. We don't want wars even when we win. We are not proud to make good soldiers. We do not rejoice in victories. We rejoice when a new kind of cotton is grown and when strawberries bloom in what was once the deserts of Israel. We have been obliged to become good soldiers, but not with joy. We are good farmers with joy.''

She spoke about what it meant to be Jewish: ''There is something not explainable, which impels Jews to go on being Jews through thick and thin. Whatever the mysterious reason, it is a historical fact that there is something in the Jewish spirit which has upheld Jewishness through the ages against all odds. Oh, always some Jews have fallen by the wayside, but by and large we have pressed forward as Jews and even in exile and martyrdom we have outlived many empires. I admit it's irrational, but it's incontestable.''

And she spoke of what Israel meant to her: ''Israel is not just some small beleaguered country, in which three million people are trying hard to survive; Israel is a Jewish state that has come into existence as the result of the longing, the faith and the determination of an ancient people. Because Israel exists Jewish history has been changed forever . . .''

Golda made these speaking trips because of her strong sense of duty. But they often exhausted her. Although her zest for life was as strong as ever, she was in her mid-seventies, and her body was beginning to rebel. Often she was stricken with blinding migraine headaches. Also, she had phlebitis—an inflammation of the veins. If she walked too far or stood in one position too long her legs felt as though they had been invaded by fiery pokers. So her spirits always lifted when she was able to head for home again.

For so many years almost every waking hour had been rigidly controlled. And most of those hours had been dedicated to the service of others. Now she was determined to live her own life. "After fifty years of public service I deserve it! Now I'm going to be private citizen Meir at last!"

Then, as often as not, she would chuckle. "Oh, I know what people have been saying. They are saying I will soon sicken and even die of boredom. But they don't know me!"

Soon after she retired Golda gave an interview. "You see," she told the reporter very seriously, "I am a lazy woman at heart . . ."

The reporter couldn't help it. She laughed out loud at this obvious absurdity. After a moment Golda, too, smiled. "Okay," she agreed. "Maybe not lazy. But you must understand, I am not really one of those people who have to fill up every minute or else gets depressed. I like to be with nothing to do, even just sitting in an armchair, or wasting time with little things I enjoy. Things like cleaning house, ironing, cooking a meal. I'm an excellent cook, you know, an excellent housewife!" Now Golda's eyes began to twinkle. "And then there's maybe the most important thing of all. Sleep! I like it so much!"

As a private person Golda did do all these simple things she'd dreamed of for so long. Of course, being Golda, she managed to do much, much more.

Once a friend decided to keep a record of Golda's activities during one week. She attended several luncheons, a wedding, a bar mitzvah, a diplomatic dinner, a poetry reading, a play at the National Theater of Israel, and a folk dancing exhibition. All this she squeezed in between Monday morning and midday Friday. Then on Friday afternoon she packed a small bag and set off to do what she, as an old kibbutznik herself, loved most of all—to spend the weekend at her daughter Sarah's kibbutz in the heart of the Negev Desert.

Golda was now a private citizen. For more than three years she'd had little or nothing to do with affairs of state. But suddenly she was catapulted into the center of world affairs once more.

It began when President Anwar el Sadat of Egypt announced, "I am ready to go to the end of the world to get a peace settlement with Israel. I am even ready to go to the Knesset, and speak to all the members of the Israeli parliament there and negotiate with them over a true settlement."

All around Israel Jews read this amazing statement in their newspapers and muttered, "Ani lo ma'amin." *I don't believe it!*

Golda found it just as hard to believe. She and Sadat had been deadly foes. So often they had sat in war-rooms plotting each other's destruction.

Golda also remembered some of Sadat's statements. "A showdown with Israel is inevitable and I am prepared to sacrifice a million men," he proclaimed. He also said, "There is no call holier than the call to war." And, "The problem is not to blockade this or blockade that. The problem is how to totally exterminate the State of Israel for all time."

"So what's made the leopard change his spots?" one Israeli asked.

The answer was simple. Anwar Sadat was a realist, a very practical man. And his country was in deep economic trouble. A great many people were unemployed, and prices for everything were skyrocketing.

To make matters worse, Sadat, and Nasser before him, had fought and lost four very expensive wars with Israel. Now, because of the ever-present tension between the two countries, he had to continue spending huge amounts of money for armaments. The simple answer was that the less hostility there was between his country and Israel the better life would be for the average Egyptian.

So at 8 P.M. on November 19, 1977, the whole world watched as the Egyptian President's official jet swept out of the night sky and roared to a stop on the runway at Ben-Gurion Airport. The flight had taken just thirty minutes. "A minute for every year of bloodshed," Golda thought as she waited with the other Israeli dignitaries to greet their long-time enemy.

Prime Minister Menachem Begin and President

Sadat stood at rigid attention as the two national anthems were played and a twenty-one-gun salute boomed in the visitor's honor. Then Sadat began to make his way down the line of waiting Israelis. The mood was friendly—but very serious. Then he came to Golda, and the expression on his face softened a little.

"I have waited a long time to see you," he said, as he shook her hand.

"Mr. President," Golda answered, her every word weighted with meaning, "I, too, have been waiting a long time to see you!"

"Well, here I am!" Sadat answered almost gaily. Then he kissed Golda on the cheek.

The same warm mood continued between the two old foes. Two days later Sadat met with the members of the Labor Party. Golda, as its most important ex-leader, sat beside him.

For so many years Anwar Sadat had been a firm believer in the Arabs' basic policy against Israel. No peace. No recognition. No negotiations.

Now he was daring to break with this futile pattern of the three no's. And Golda applauded him for it. "Direct contact is infinitely preferable to contact through intermediaries," she said very firmly. "So let us at least conclude one thing: the beginning you made with such courage and with such hope for peace, it must go on, face to face, between us and you . . ."

Golda paused, as if searching for still more solemn words. But just as she could be direct and blunt, she also found it easy to be very human. Now her eyes began to dance as she continued. "Yes, it must go on between us so that even an old lady like *me* will live to see the day!"

For a moment President Sadat looked embarrassed. How many times in the past he had called Golda "that old lady!" And he had certainly not meant it as a compliment. But then he saw the mischievous expression on Golda's face and he began to laugh.

"Oh, yes, Mr. President," Golda concluded sweetly. "I know you always called me 'that old lady.' " Now she held out a small gift-wrapped present. A few days before, Sadat's first grandchild had been born in Egypt.

"Well, as a grandmother to a grandfather, I give this to you," she said warmly. Now everyone in the room was smiling. Once more Golda, with her sense of humanity and humor, had stolen the show.

In the spring of 1978 Golda celebrated her eightieth birthday. A few years before, a reporter had asked her how she felt about the subject of death. Golda answered quickly, for this was something she'd given some thought to. "My only fear is to live too long," she answered. "You know, old age is not a sin and not a joy—there are plenty of disagreeable things about old age. Yet you get used to some things without difficulty. Physical troubles aren't degrading. My only fear is that I may lose my mental lucidity. Yes, I want to die with my mind clear."

Golda paused, then smiled a little. "My dear, I

think it's like this. Old age is like an airplane flying in a storm. Once you're in it, there's nothing you can do. You can't stop a plane, you can't stop a storm, you can't stop time. So you might as well take it easy, with wisdom.''

Golda knew what she was talking about. She had always been an expert at keeping secrets—both public and private. But very soon her own best-kept secret would be revealed to the world.

For twelve years Golda had been fighting a great private battle against leukemia—a cancerous disease of the blood. She had continued to live as if spirit were stronger than flesh—and kept the disease at bay.

But now the fight was almost over. All through the summer and fall she grew weaker. On December 8, 1978, Golda Meir was dead. A shock wave of mourning swept around the world. As a close friend said, ''She was so much more than just a leader. She was the mother of us all, and a universal Kaddish''—the prayer usually said only for close relatives—''went up as she was laid to rest among the creators, builders and dreamers of the Jewish state.''

Golda had always lived a simple life. She was determined that her death would be just as plain. Famous people and world leaders usually have very fancy funerals—full of pomp and ceremony. Golda wanted none of that. So she left some instructions.

There were two things that she specifically asked for. She wanted to be buried in a plain pine coffin. And she wanted no eulogies given around her grave—no speeches full of long, windy, and often empty, words of praise.

But Golda's death had filled so many people —Jews and non-Jews—with an aching sense of loss.

"She spoke to everyone the same way," Israel's Ambassador to the United States said.

"Golda's life represented not only the history of an individual but of a people," Secretary of State Henry Kissinger wrote. "She showed an extraordinary integration of tremendous power and humanness."

"I am saddened by the passing of a first class political leader and an honest foe," announced Anwar Sadat.

"Her name will live forever in Jewish history."

"An inspiration . . ."

"A giant among us, larger than life . . ."

Perhaps a young kibbutznik, younger than Golda had been when she first set foot in Jewish Palestine, best and most simply put into words what Golda's life and death meant to so many. "Today, suddenly," she said, "the world has become a much less extraordinary place."

Some people did not put their grief into words. They found other ways to mourn. Some cried. Some prayed in synagogues around the world. Golda's body lay in state outside the Knesset for three days before the funeral. Day and night long lines of Israelis inched past, saying their last silent good-byes.

Suddenly an elderly man stepped out of line. He went up to a member of the honor guard standing at attention beside Golda's coffin and spoke to him.

At first the guard frowned and shook his head. Then the man pulled a worn snapshot out of his pocket. It was a picture of himself and Golda. It had been taken long ago when they'd stood and fought side by side as *chaverim*—comrades—in the struggle to make Israel a nation.

The guard looked at the picture for several moments. He hesitated—then nodded yes. The old man moved to the side of the coffin. For five minutes he stood there stiffly at attention. Then he reached down, touched the coffin lightly, and moved quietly away. He was content, for he had said his own special good-bye to Golda, his old friend.

A Note to My Readers

If you read other books about Golda, you will probably notice that some of the names of her family, friends, and acquaintances may be spelled a little differently than here. For example Golda's older sister's name is usually spelled Shaina, as it is here. But it has also been spelled Shana, Sheina, and Sheyna. There is a reason for this. These names were originally written in the Hebrew alphabet—an alphabet very different from the one we are familiar with. When the names were translated into English, one person would spell them one way, and another a slightly different way. But you will notice if you say one of these names aloud—Shana, Sheina, Sheyna, or Shaina, for example—the different spellings will all sound alike.

M. D.

Bibliography
A Partial Listing

Agress, Eliyahu. *Golda Meir: Portrait of a Prime Minister*. New York: Sabra Books, 1969.

Ben-Gurion, David. *Memoirs*. New York: World Publishing Company, 1970.

Dimont, Max. *Jews, God, and History*. New York: Simon and Schuster, 1962.

Elon, Amos. *The Israelis, Founders and Sons*. New York: Holt, Rinehart & Winston, Inc., 1971.

Golden, Harry. *The Israelis*. New York: G. P. Putnam's Sons, 1971.

Grayzel, Solomon. *A History of the Jews*. New York: Mentor Books, 1947.

Gruber, Ruth. *Israel on the Seventh Day*. New York: Hill and Wang, 1968.

Korngold, Shaina. *Memories*. Translated from Hebrew, 1968.

Mann, Peggy. *Golda, The Life of Israel's Prime Minister*. New York: Coward, McCann and Geoghegan, 1972.

Meir, Golda. *A Land of Our Own, An Oral Autobiography,* edited by Marie Syrkin. New York: G. P. Putnam's Sons, 1973.

————. *This Is Our Strength,* edited by Henry M. Christman. New York: Macmillan, 1962.

————. *My Life*. New York: G. P. Putnam's Sons, 1975.

Pool, de Sola, David. *Why I Am a Jew*. Thomas Nelson and Sons, 1957.

Roth, Cecil, *A History of the Jews: From Earliest Times Through the Six Day War*. New York: Schocken Books, 1954.

Shenker, Israel and Mary, eds. *As Good as Golda: The Warmth and Wisdom of Israel's Prime Minister*. New York: McCall Publishing, 1970.

Stern, Mrs. Clara. *Personal Interviews Concerning Her Sister Golda,* in Hartford, Connecticut, 1974.

Suhl, Yuri. *They Fought Back*. New York: Crown Publishers, Inc., 1968.

Syrkin, Marie. *Way of Valor*. New York: Sheron Books, 1955.

————. *Woman With a Cause*. New York: G. P. Putnam's Sons, 1963.

————. *Golda Meir, Israel's Leader*. New York: G. P. Putnam's Sons, 1969.

Zborowski, Mark, and Herzog, Elizabeth. *Life Is With People: The Culture of the Shtetl*. New York: Schocken Books, 1952.

Zionist Archives, *Magazine and Newspaper Articles*. New York City.

Index

Pledge of Allegiance to the Flag, 66
Poale Zion, 125, 128
Pocahontas (ship), 128
Pogroms, 24–26, 110, 136
 meaning of, 7–8
Poland, 44–46, 51, 110
Prime Minister's Mansion (Jerusalem), 196
Proclamation of Independence (Israel), 178–180

Radio Cairo, 198
Rhodesia, 193
Roman Empire, 113
Romania, 110, 194
Roosevelt, Franklin D., 150
Rosh Hashanah, 187
Russia, 1–42, 43, 44, 72, 110, 194
 border crossing to Poland, 44–46
 hatred of Jews, 110
 near pogroms, 1–9
 Pale of Settlement, 11, 17
 special permits for Jews in, 11, 17

Sabbath, 29–31, 33, 78–79, 141
 preparations for, 29
 tradition to invite the poor, 31
Sabbath Eve meal, 30–31, 79
Sabra, 144
Sadat, President Anwar el, first visit to Israel, 215–218
St. Petersburg, Russia, 25
Saudi Arabia, King of, 166
Schnorrer, 172
Shertok, Moshe, 180
Siberia, 38
Socialism, 102
Switzerland, international conference at (1938), 150–152
Syria, 120, 181, 182

Talmud, 20
Tel-Aviv, Israel, 133–135, 148, 181, 196
Tel-Aviv Airport, 169
Tel-Aviv Art Museum, 178
Trade unionism, 102
Trans-Jordan, 172–175, 181, 183
Turkey, 120
Turkish Empire, 124
Turkish Jews, 189

Ukraine, 11
Uncle Tom's Cabin, 69–71, 131
Unions, 31, 57, 102
United Nations, 163–164, 165, 167, 173, 189, 193, 194

Valley of Jezreel, 137
Victoria Falls, 193

World War I, 109–111, 126
World War II, 152–153, 156–157

Yarmulkas, 187
Yehudith (housekeeper), 194
Yemen, 190
Yiddish language, 7, 13, 55, 56, 64, 83–84, 97, 172, 186, 188
Yom-Kippur War, *see* Arab-Israel War of 1973
Young Maccabean, The (magazine), 113

Zambia, independence of, 193
Zionism, 102, 152, 159
 basic aim of, 118–119
 Golda's streetcorner speech on, 109–117
 Palestine Bank Accounts for, 118–132
 purpose of, 113

Temple Israel

Minneapolis, Minnesota

In Honor of the Bar Mitzvah of
BILL WOLFSON
by
Fremajane, Blair & Robby Wolfson
December 10, 1983